Virtual Learning Environments

Virtual Learning Environments considers how VLEs can be successfully deployed and used for effective teaching in universities and colleges. It sets out a model for effective use and seeks to provide a bridge between pedagogical approaches and the tools educators have at their disposal. Considering e-learning in its broadest context, including blended and distance learning, *Virtual Leaning Environments* covers the following key issues:

- the context within which VLEs are operating
- how they can be used to support different teaching approaches
- methodology for selecting and reviewing VLEs
- the issues surrounding the implementation of a VLE, including interaction with other university systems
- personalization in VLEs and how software can influence behaviour
- the process of technology succession and the influence of open content

Illustrated by case studies which highlight the different requirements and approaches of diverse institutions, *Virtual Learning Environments* provides advice for those choosing a VLE and encourages all those involved in the deployment of VLEs to use them more productively in order to create engaging learning experiences. It is essential reading for policy and decision makers, e-learning champions and support staff, technical developers and educators.

Martin Weller is Professor of Educational Technology at the Open University, where he was Director of the VLE project.

Virtual Learning Environments

Using, choosing and developing your VLE

Martin Weller

Routledge
Taylor & Francis Group
LONDON AND NEW YORK

First published 2007
by Routledge
2 Park Square, Milton Park, Abingdon, Oxon, OX14 4RN

Simultaneously published in the USA and Canada
by Routledge
270 Madison Ave, New York, NY 10016

Routledge is an imprint of the Taylor and Francis Group, an informa business

Typeset in Times New Roman and Gill Sans by
Florence Production Ltd, Stoodleigh, Devon
Printed and bound in Great Britain by
TJ International Ltd, Padstow, Cornwall

British Library Cataloguing in Publication Data
A catalogue record for this book is available from the British Library

Library of Congress Cataloging in Publication Data
Weller, Martin.
Virtual learning environments: using, choosing and developing your VLE/ Martin Weller.
p. cm.
Includes bibliographical references and index.
1. Computer-assisted instruction. 2. Internet in education. I. Title.
LB1028.5.W3946 2007
371.33'4–dc22 2006027550

ISBN10: 0–415–41430–X (hbk)
ISBN10: 0–415–41431–8 (pbk)
ISBN10: 0–203–96434–9 (ebk)

ISBN13: 978–0–415–41430–2 (hbk)
ISBN13: 978–0–415–41431–9 (pbk)
ISBN13: 978–0–203–96434–7 (ebk)

To John Naughton, from whom I learnt the only career advice worth following – do interesting things.

Contents

Figures

Preface

Most higher education institutions now have some form of virtual learning environment. Often these have been acquired without a clear idea as to what they were intended to achieve or how they would influence current practice. This first raft of implementation has provided invaluable experience in both the technological aspects (such as how to integrate a VLE with current university systems) and teaching (such as how they can best be used to support learners). But nothing stands still, and in both of these areas things have moved on since the initial VLE decision was made. With exposure to existing VLEs many academics have begun to see the possibilities in the technology and to ask more of the system. Similarly students have become accustomed to institution-wide use of systems to disseminate information, and to engage in dialogue with their peers and educators. On the technical front a number of developments have seen systems become more standardized and interoperable.

Much of the first wave of VLE implementation was done at a local level, with different schools and faculties deploying different systems. As e-learning becomes a mainstream activity for most institutions and for some central to their strategic direction, the significance and profile of the VLE has risen. There has been a subsequent shift to making VLEs an institution-wide system.

Thus many institutions are now in a review phase where they consider their current VLE provision and e-learning practice. They are seeking to position e-learning in their overall provision and strategy, and simultaneously evaluating their technology and its ability to meet their expected needs.

The aim of this book is twofold. The first aim is to help inform the various people involved in this e-learning review process. This audience includes policy and decision makers, e-learning champions and support staff, technical developers, and educators with an interest in e-learning.

The second aim is more theoretical. There are a number of themes and developments in higher education currently which converge around the role of e-learning and educational technology. For example the nature of assessment and what we assess, the role of partnerships, the student experience, the nature of the course, the type of resources used and the underlying business models of higher education all find an expression in, and are challenged by, e-learning developments. Thus the manner in which a VLE is chosen, how it is deployed and what the future directions are for VLE development act as a proxy for many of these debates. The second aim of this book then is to explore the issues surrounding VLEs as a reflection of more general trends.

The book sets out the context within which VLEs are operating (Chapters 1 and 2), how they can be used to support different teaching approaches (Chapters 3 and 4) and methodology for selecting and reviewing VLEs (Chapter 5). Chapters 6 to 9 are concerned with the issues surrounding the implementation of a VLE, looking at the systems a VLE needs to interact with to form a managed learning environment (MLE), the emerging educational technology standards, and the debate between open source and commercial VLEs. Chapters 10 and 11 look at some more theoretical issues, regarding personalization in VLEs and the manner in which software can influence behaviour. Chapter 12 provides some case studies and Chapter 13 sets these in the context of the process of technology succession. Lastly, Chapter 14 looks at possible future directions by considering the influence of two current developments, namely web 2.0 and open content. It also suggests a number of research themes for VLEs in the coming years.

While some sections of the book may appeal to certain audiences more than others I have attempted to provide something for everyone in all chapters. Most chapters therefore end with a general discussion around the broader issues, so even some of the more technical chapters such as those on MLEs and standards have something to offer the general reader.

Acknowledgements

The basis for this book arose out of the research and work I did as the Director for the VLE project at the UK Open University. My first round of thanks then go to those associated with that project, in particular Paul Clark for appointing me to the role, Dean Taylor for providing such capable support and all the members of the project team for their input and guidance.

I am based in the Institute of Educational Technology at the Open University, which provides an excellent environment for research and discussion. My gratitude goes to my colleagues there, especially the Director Peter Knight for allowing me the time to complete this book and Patrick McAndrew who suggested I write it.

A number of people provided advice and input to specific chapters, including Robin Mason, Chris Pegler, Thanh Le, Ross Mackenzie, Adam Joinson, Non Scantlebury and Gràinne Conole. Externally to the OU, James Dalziel, Charles Severance, Rob Koper and the OUTEC team at the OU Netherlands and the VLE team at Deakin University also helped inform my writing on particular subjects.

Lastly, thanks go to my wife, Sarah, for feigning appropriate interest when I talked about subjects such as service oriented architectures, and my daughter, Ellen, for rightly admonishing me when I had spent too long on the 'pongcuter'.

Abbreviations

ADL	Advanced Distributed Learning
API	application programming interface
BSD	Berkeley Software Distribution
CMS	course management system/content management system
CSCL	computer-supported collaborative learning
EML	Educational Modelling Language
FE	further education
GUI	graphical user interface
HE	higher education
ICT	information and communication technology
IM	instant messaging
IPR	intellectual property rights
JISC	Joint Information Systems Committee
LAMS	Learning Activity Management System
LCMS	learning content management system
LD	Learning Design
LIP	Learner Information Package
LMS	learning management system
LOM	Learning Object Metadata
MCQ	multiple choice question
MLE	managed learning environment
OCW	Open Courseware initiative
OER	open educational resources
OKI	Open Knowledge Initiative
PDA	personal digital assistants
PDP	personal development planning
PLE	personal learning environment
QTI	Question & Test Interoperability
RFP	request for proposal
RSS	Really Simple Syndication/Rich Site Summary
SCORM	Sharable Content Object Reference Model
SLeD	Service-based Learning Design

SOAP	Simple Object Access Protocol
UDDI	Universal Description, Discovery and Integration
UML	Unified Modelling Language
VLE	virtual learning environment
VRE	virtual research environment
WAI	Web Accessibility Initiative
WSDL	Web Services Description Language
XML	Extensible Markup Language

Chapter 1

What we talk about when we talk about e-learning

E-learning produces more angst and enthusiasm than can be consumed locally, so it tends to spill over into other areas. One could draw a complex Venn diagram with e-learning intersecting with other topics in education, including lifelong learning, increased educational demand, education in developing countries, the nature of assessment, the role of the academic, commercialization in education, intellectual property and flexibility in education. And then there is the overlap with broader technological developments such as open source software, web services integration techniques, educational technology standards, the semantic web, etc. And underlying all of these activities is the environment in which e-learning takes place, the VLE or LMS (see below for a discussion on terminology). The pedagogical, political, technical and economical arguments that pervade e-learning are all reflected in the choice, deployment and development of a VLE in an organization.

Unsurprisingly the issues which proliferate around e-learning lead to confusion, resentment and sometimes disdain from many educators. Their job, and inclination, is to teach and research in their subject and remain up to date in that field, not to continually develop new skills in using technologies or become experts in educational theory, XML programming and educational technology standards. As these areas develop rapidly the energy required to keep up with them becomes an increasing drain on the resources of any academic. What many enthusiasts, government officials and managers often fail to appreciate is that an educator's time (and interest) is a finite resource; if one occupies it with one area it is at the detriment of another. If they engage with e-learning at all, then the feeling many educators have is one of bewilderment and confusion, akin to that of Einstein, who, lost on his way to a meeting, telephoned his wife Elsa and asked, 'Where am I? And where *should* I be?'

Rather like the *Hitchhiker's Guide to the Galaxy*, the message of this book is 'Don't Panic'. The presence of a VLE in your institution is the means by which you can engage effectively with these issues. It won't make you understand educational theory, and it won't change your institution overnight, but by adopting a few simple principles and working with these fairly straightforward systems, much of the rest will follow of its own accord. For instance, you don't need to be an expert in assessment methods and policy to realize that you can use online assessment to reinforce and motivate students, that you can then move beyond standard multiple choice questions to achieve this and that maybe you want to capture some of the discussion in your end of course assessment in a way that is lost in an exam.

This is not a book just about technology, it is about the effective application of that technology. VLEs are perhaps not the most innovative technology in recent years, but they are one of the most pervasive in higher education with 86 per cent of respondents from UK higher education (HE) institutions reporting the presence of a VLE in their institution (Brown and Jenkins 2003) and 70 per cent of UK further education (FE) colleges using a proprietary VLE (Becta 2004). As such they represent something of a Trojan horse that has slipped into most institutions almost unnoticed. This book is about the nature of the technology and the issues surrounding it, for it is not an exaggeration to say that to understand these is to understand most of the issues facing higher education currently.

In this chapter we will firstly look at the definitions and terminology associated with VLEs, and then turn our attention to the context within which VLEs operate. It is impossible to consider the effective use of VLEs without taking into account the broader e-learning context, as this shapes many people's reactions to the technology and how it is to be used. It is therefore worthwhile drawing out some of the issues and framing the technology.

What's in a name?

First let us turn to the issue of terminology and definition. As with most new terms, there is little agreement as to which term one should use for an online learning environment, and still less agreement as to what one actually is and where its boundaries with other systems lie. There is also a fair degree of hostility to certain terms and the possible implications they carry.

The term virtual learning environment is often objected to because of the 'virtual', as it seems to be in contrast to 'real', which implies that learning through such an environment is a poor relation to any learning that takes place in a face-to-face setting. Anyone who has sat through tedious lectures from disinterested lecturers will know this is patently not the case, but nevertheless there is that suggestion in the term.

Similarly, 'learning management system' (LMS) causes consternation in some educators because of the suggestion that it 'manages' the student's learning in a very direct manner. This is somewhat at odds with the more exploratory, constructivist teaching approaches that many favour in e-learning, and seems more suitable in a training context.

Definitions can be in terms of functionality, for instance Whatis.com states

> The principal components of a VLE package include curriculum mapping (breaking curriculum into sections that can be assigned and assessed), student tracking, online support for both teacher and student, electronic communication (e-mail, threaded discussions, chat, Web publishing), and Internet links to outside curriculum resources.

A popular definition is that provided by the Joint Information Systems Committee (JISC 2000) in the UK, which states the term VLE refers to 'the components in which learners and tutors participate in "on-line" interactions of various kinds, including on-line learning'.

An LMS is defined by Whatis.com as

> a software application or Web-based technology used to plan, implement, and assess a specific learning process. Typically, a learning management system provides an instructor with a way to create and deliver content, monitor student participation, and assess student performance. A learning management system may also provide students with the ability to use interactive features such as threaded discussions, video conferencing, and discussion forums.

Paulsen (2002) suggests that LMS is 'a broad term that is used for a wide range of systems that organize and provide access to online learning services for students, teachers, and administrators. These services usually include access control, provision of learning content, communication tools, and organizations of user groups.'

Another term, which can be taken as synonymous with VLE and LMS, is course management system. This is particularly confusing because the acronym CMS is the same as that for another type of system found in e-learning, namely content management systems (which we will look at in Chapter 6). Content management systems *are* different from VLEs. A qualification to this is made by some by the addition of 'learning' to make learning content management systems (LCMS). This is sometimes used to mean a system for storing learning content, and at other times as synonymous with VLE.

To further complicate matters the term MLE (managed learning environment) has also come into popular usage, and sometimes the terms VLE, LMS and course management systems are all grouped together under this term. Generally an MLE is taken to encompass all university systems, not just those that focus specifically on the learning process, but administrative systems such as student records. JISC (2000) defines an MLE as 'The whole range of information systems and processes of an institution (including a VLE if appropriate) that contribute directly, or indirectly, to learning and the management of that learning.'

How an MLE is constructed will vary between organizations, based partly on the existing systems, such as the student record system, and also the preferred integration method of the technical staff. One such arrangement is shown in Figure 1.1.

While such diagrams are useful to convey an impression of complex software systems, anyone who has tried to delineate the boundaries between such systems will know that boxes and arrows greatly simplify a messy reality. We will look at the relationship between VLEs and other systems in Chapter 6.

There is also some geographical preference for terms, with LMS being more prevalent in the US, and VLE favoured in Europe, and the terms used interchangeably in other countries.

While we should not underestimate the importance of semantics and terminology, my inclination is to take a pragmatic approach to these issues. One can go too far down a linguistic deterministic route by stressing the manner in which labels will determine how people use a technology, which underestimates most users' ability to see the technology in its own right and think about its application to their context. Debates around terminology and definitions often generate more heat than light, their length and ferocity almost indirectly proportional to their usefulness. So while all of the current

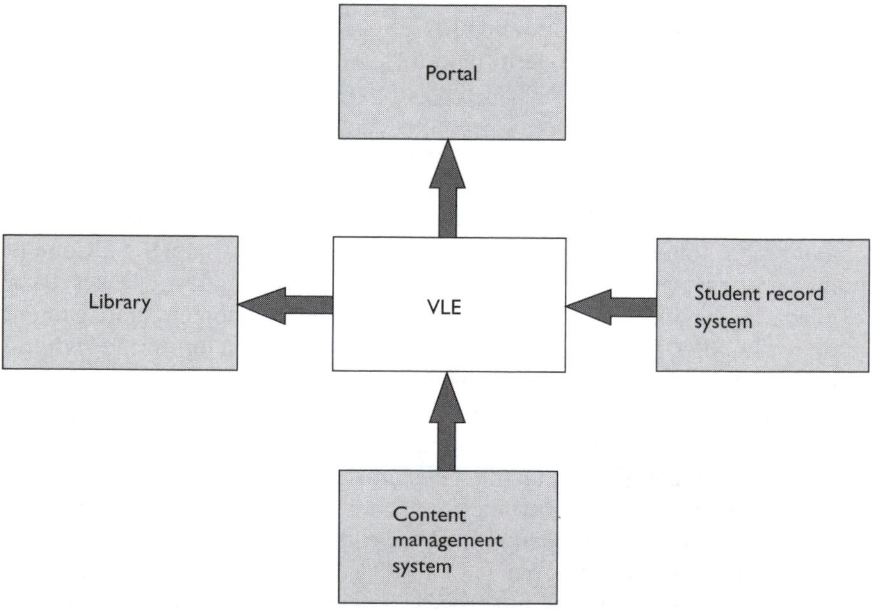

Figure 1.1 An MLE combines all the systems that are relevant to learning, with a VLE being a subset of these.

terms are flawed in some respects, they are at least widely used and generally understood. Rather than switch between them, in this book I will opt for VLE, simply because it is the term I have become accustomed to, but for the purposes of this book you should consider VLE and LMS to be synonymous. For our purposes, we will define a VLE and LMS as 'a software system that combines a number of different tools that are used to systematically deliver content online and facilitate the learning experience around that content'.

This definition is sufficiently broad to encompass most recognized VLEs, regardless of whether they have an underlying pedagogy associated with them. It does, however, deliberately exclude bespoke websites, or specific tools that may be used in a learning context but do not in themselves constitute a VLE. The point about a VLE is that it is an enterprise, institution-wide system used by a variety of educators to deliver a range of courses; it is not specific to one course or one function. We will look at what VLEs offer and the dimensions to their functionality in a later chapter, but for now this definition and, more importantly, your instinctive feeling as to what one is, are sufficient.

The purpose of any VLE is to facilitate e-learning, so I should set out a definition of that term also. The US-based *Learning Circuits* magazine (http://www.learningcircuits.org/glossary) defines it as 'a wide set of applications and processes, such as Web-based learning, computer-based learning, virtual classrooms, and digital collaboration. It includes the delivery of content via internet, intranet/extranet (LAN/WAN), audio- and videotape, satellite broadcast, interactive TV, CD-ROM, and more.'

Such broad definitions would take into account an individual working alone with a CD-ROM, and also students working collaboratively online. However, it was through the rise of the Internet that the 'e' prefix came into popular usage, and in line with e-commerce, e-business and e-government, it is the internet that is really the defining technology in e-learning. What is different about e-learning is the online aspect, and if any institution is to tackle the fundamental issues that e-learning raises for education, it needs to focus on the particular characteristics of the internet, rather than any and all use of information and communications technology (ICT). CD-ROMs have been in use by students for many years, but because these are offline and follow a standard publishing model they do not address the issues that the internet raises – they essentially perform the same function as books. So, for the purpose of this book I will define e-learning as any learning experience that utilizes internet-related technologies to some extent. This definition emphasizes the internet as the primary medium with regards to e-learning but does not exclude blending with other media and approaches (for example DVD, face-to-face, print, etc.), but by focusing on the internet, some key features of the medium, and how these relate to learning and teaching can be examined.

The e-learning debate

I mentioned at the outset that e-learning excites much debate, hype and anxiety amongst educators, probably more than any other topic. Whilst it is not the purpose of this book to analyse the political and financial climate in which e-learning is being promoted and resisted, it is worth considering what it is about the application of the internet to learning that generates such strong feelings.

This debate arises from two fundamentally differing views of the internet and how it can best be deployed in education. Let us call these the broadcast and the discussion viewpoints. For the e-learning detractors, who see e-learning as a means of commoditizing education, deprofessionalizing the educator and commercializing universities, the internet is a broadcast medium. In this world the educator is replaced by content, which can be reused and accessed by many. The internet is an unprecedented delivery mechanism because it can deliver content globally and at the user's demand. One of the current debates in e-learning has been around the concept of learning objects, which seems to endorse this broadcast, content-focused viewpoint for many. It should also be noted that those who view the internet as a cost-effective means of delivering learning (for example much of corporate training) would also adhere to the broadcast view.

For e-learning enthusiasts the internet is an unprecedented communication medium. Central to this viewpoint is the concept of the internet facilitating *two-way* communication. The internet encourages discussion, dialogue and community in a manner that is not limited by time or place. The role of educators in this world is to facilitate dialogue and support students in their understanding of resources.

The reason these two viewpoints have been proposed here is that they lead to profoundly different approaches as to how the internet is employed in education and also the extent to which it is adopted. In broad pedagogical terms the broadcast worldview leads to an instructivist approach and the discussion worldview leads to a constructivist one. There are many more approaches than this simple classification would imply, as we will see in Chapter 3, but they do represent the two main pedagogical camps as they relate to e-learning. It is worth appreciating that these two pedagogical approaches are a consequence of deeper beliefs regarding the nature of the technology itself, which are often not articulated. Because e-learning evokes such strong feelings, it often forces people into one of these two camps which are then positioned as being mutually exclusive.

This potentially represents a problem for any institution that wishes to really grasp the potential of e-learning. For example the broadcast viewpoint has been characterized as a belief that 'content is king' which ignores the educational importance of dialogue (both between students and with an educator). This creates a reaction in those who subscribe to the discussion viewpoint, which places an emphasis on dialogue and collaboration which in turn underestimates the importance of good quality content.

This also suggests why the internet has generated a qualitatively different reaction amongst educators than almost any other educational technology. CD-ROMs, video cassettes, computer assisted learning packages and simulations have all come (and to some extent gone) without a great deal of anxiety. People did not suggest that multimedia CD-ROMs would cause quality higher education to 'become the exclusive preserve of the privileged, available only to children of the rich and the powerful' and consequently everyone else would be in a 'dismal new era of higher education' (Noble 1998), but the use of the internet in education elicits such prophecies of doom.

My suggestion as to why this is so, and why the internet differs from previous educational technologies, is embedded in the two viewpoints set out above. One can view any learning experience as consisting of two components – content and dialogue. These two components become obvious in an e-learning context, but they apply equally to a conventional lecture. The content will be the main body of the lecture, plus any additional material including handouts, Powerpoint files, readings, etc. The dialogue is the discussion and interaction within the lecture, and also the more informal discussion that may take place afterwards in corridors or cafes. Even when an individual is reading a book alone the two elements are present – the content in the book itself and the dialogue the reader creates with that text through the process of thinking about the content, creating questions, checking back for clarification, making notes and so on. The degree to which an element is present varies from situation to situation – a small tutorial is largely focused around dialogue, whereas reading a book is mainly content driven.

Previous technologies have almost exclusively focused on the content component of the learning equation. This does not arouse anxiety in most educators – they quite rightly assume that education is more than just content. We have had books for a very long time after all, and their presence has not reduced the need for universities (quite the opposite in fact). The internet, however, is an excellent medium for both content delivery *and* dialogue. This is why it is perceived by some as more of a threat and why resistance to its uptake is more entrenched, as it potentially encroaches upon the domain of educators. There is, of course, no reason why this need be the case – educators can be equally effective in terms of the content they deliver and the dialogue they foster in this medium as any other, but it does require them to consider both aspects.

The solution to a good e-learning experience then is no magical formula, but it simply relies on the combination of these two elements. By creating good content and fostering meaningful dialogue the two ingredients for learning are present, and just as importantly the educator is respecting and acknowledging the attributes of the medium they are working within.

Expanding higher education

The number of students entering higher education is increasing globally. According to Goddard (1998) the demand for higher education is expanding exponentially throughout the world and by 2025 as many as 150 million people will be seeking higher education. This can be seen as the result of changes in career profiles (the demise of the job for life concept means people frequently need to reskill), global politics (an increase in higher education often accompanies democracy) and a global knowledge economy (people are not restricted to local employment markets). This is sometimes accompanied by political directives, for instance in 1999 Tony Blair announced a target of 50 per cent of young adults going into HE in the UK by 2010. Even without this target an increase in the number of 18- to 22-year-olds is likely to mean a further 87,000 students in UK HE by 2010.

Similarly, the Chinese Government set a target of 15 per cent of 18- to 22-year-olds to enter HE by 2010, but this target looks to have been achieved already, representing some 16 million students. When one considers that as recently as 1997 that figure was around 3.2 million students, it demonstrates a rapid expansion. Worldwide, student numbers grew at 3.9 per cent per year in the 1990s, with expansion markedly higher in developing countries.

In the US the numbers are similarly expanding, but the expansion is in a different demographic, with the number of students who are older than 24 exceeding those in the traditional core student age range of 18 to 22 for the first time. This may indicate that the younger market has reached saturation, but there is still a considerable demand for HE in an older age range. The same is true in the UK, with more than 50 per cent of students classified as 'mature'. However, there is some evidence that demand will peak, especially in developed countries; for example Australia saw rapid expansion in the 1990s, but this seems to have levelled off (Martin and Karmel 2002).

Martin Amis (2003: 8) wrote of fame that it had 'so democratized itself that obscurity was felt as a deprivation or even a punishment'. The same now seems true of participation in higher education. Many have suggested that e-learning is the only way to cope with this expansion, as physical campuses struggle to cope, for example the commercial VLE company WebCT (2003) claimed that 'E-Learning technology is a proven way to expand an institution's enrollment capacity without the capital outlays for new construction. Institutional infrastructure can be built virtually rather than physically, often at lower cost.'

E-learning is not necessarily the only means of coping with expanding higher education – if face-to-face education was absolutely demanded as the sole approach, then sufficient mechanisms could be found to accommodate the increased demand. However, with the change in demographics, it may be that e-learning represents at least the most convenient option, particularly for certain groups, for example postgraduates who, often encumbered with student debt, need to work while they continue their studies. It also represents a viable method for many institutions to offer distance, or at least blended, solutions which combine online and face-to-face delivery.

My point is rather more prosaic, and it is this – given that VLEs have become a pervasive technology in higher education institutions, then this increase in student numbers means that there will be a lot of people using this software over the coming years.

And a related point to bear in mind is that use of learning environments is unlike the use of many other software packages and many of its demands are different from those of other online experiences. While there are a host of good design principles (for example Jakob Nielsen's site http://www.useit.com/) for commercial websites, where you may want to attract people in and give them very immediate information, an online learning experience in contrast occurs in an environment where a student may spend several weeks, months, years even. Therefore design principles that make sense when capturing a large audience may not be applicable when you want people to engage in learning. If one considers the range in subject areas and teaching approaches then the demands on any one system to meet all of these becomes apparent. Is a tool for new students on a widening participation programme studying computer gaming the same system as one for part-time postgraduate students studying Renaissance art?

There are two approaches to this problem. The first is to develop a system that is broad enough to meet the needs of all students, and the second is to develop a range of tools that meet the needs of specific audiences. Most commercial VLEs are instances of the first (although they are expandable so that new tools can be incorporated), while newer initiatives tend to favour the latter. Wilbert Kraan (2004) of the UK standards body CETIS claims that

> It is becoming clear that common e-learning activities . . . can't really be done by one application that has little or no knowledge of everything else on the network or the wider internet. It's also becoming clearer that a single system that tries to combine all such functions is unlikely to do all of them equally well. Furthermore, one size systems do not necessarily fit all institutions.

This can be seen as the fundamental debate in the VLE field at the moment. We will look at this in some more detail in the next chapter.

Chapter 2

VLEs, democrats and revolutionaries

Technology adoption

The seminal work in the adoption of technology is Rogers' (1962) *Diffusion of Innovations*. In it he describes the manner in which innovations have an S-shaped curve of adoption, shown in Figure 2.1.

The gradient of the curve can vary, depending on the innovation in question (the innovation needn't be technological, but the pattern and categories often apply to the uptake of a technology), and factors such as how much benefit or commercial advantage it provides, the audience in which it is being adopted, the ease with which it can be adopted, and so on. The key point is that there is usually a period where the innovation is used by a relatively small community, and then as it enters the steep part of the curve uptake increases dramatically. This is also characterized as the 'tipping point', when an innovation gains a critical mass of users. There is also a flattening off of the curve, which suggests that, beyond a certain point, a lot of time (and usually resource) is required to increase the number of users.

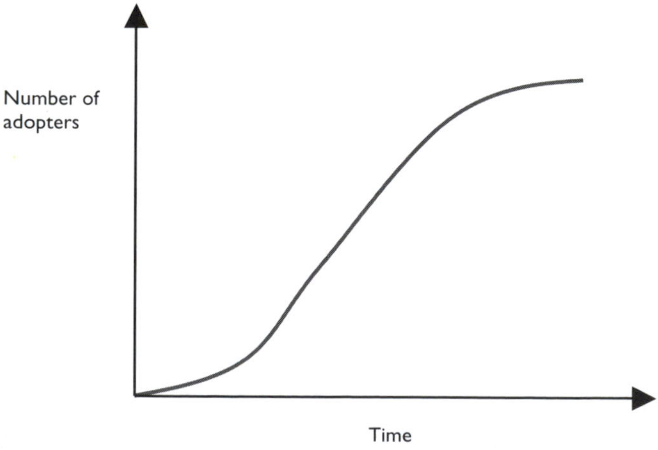

Figure 2.1 Rogers' S-shaped curve of innovation diffusion.

Rogers suggests five categories of attitude towards innovation, which are now part of common parlance:

1 innovators;
2 early adopters;
3 early majority;
4 late majority; and
5 laggards.

Rogers' theory has been adapted and modified by many others, but it remains a convenient model for both predicting and analysing the adoption of any innovation, particularly technological ones.

Similarly, Riggs and von Hippel (1994) looked at innovations developed by users and those by manufacturers. They found that innovations by users generally enabled instruments to do new things, while those by manufacturers allowed users to do the same thing but more conveniently or reliably. Von Hippel (2005) goes on to differentiate between 'lead users' and more conventional users. Lead users are often ahead of market trends, and expect to gain relatively high benefits from a solution to the needs they have encountered there. They tend to modify products, and seek out products that can be modified. These modifications in turn benefit others, and the lead users in turn get the most benefit from any modifications.

Greller (2005) suggests that if we take the standard normal distribution curve and plot innovation along the x-axis and number of staff on the y-axis (Figure 2.2), then there comes a point with many (but not all) technologies when they move beyond the early adopters, when they enter the mainstream, and at this point institutional responses kick in, typically in the form of staff development, official policy documents, and a centralization of support and resources. The technology ceases to operate as part of a cottage industry and becomes part of the mainstream – it moves toward the traditional end of the continuum. One can see this with the use of email, for example, which is now considered a mainstream technology but was once the province of enthusiasts in computer science departments. We will look at methods of promoting e-learning later, but before we leave this subject it is worth briefly considering those at the other end of this distribution curve, who Rogers labelled 'laggards'. It may be that these people will never adopt a technology (but they may have many other strengths within the organization of course), and so either workarounds are found for these people (for example a good secretary or PA), they are left out of the technology (this can be difficult if its use is mandatory, for example if email becomes the recognized method of making announcements), or compulsory measures are introduced. It is likely that different strategies and motivations will apply for these people than for those in the centre of the distribution curve.

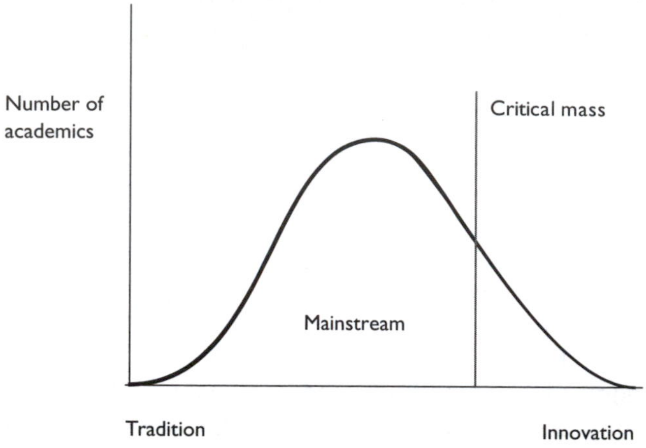

Figure 2.2 The uptake of technology within an institution follows a normal distribution curve.

The uptake of VLEs

At the start of the previous chapter I mentioned that VLEs were not the most innovative educational technology to be found in use today. This is why many researchers and educational technologists hold them in something resembling disdain. There are a number of charges often levelled at the more popular VLEs, and particularly commercial ones, which can be summarized as:

- They are content focused.
- They have no strong pedagogy.
- They are based around a teacher–classroom model.
- They combine a number of average tools, but not the best ones.
- They do not feature a particular tool.
- They operate on a lowest common denominator approach.
- They do not meet the needs of different subject areas.
- It is difficult to exchange content between them, despite claims to interoperability.

There is an element of truth in many of these claims, and we will look at some of them in more detail when we look at ways of using VLEs, but the problems they represent are not as catastrophic to successful e-learning as many of their proponents suggest.

There is something very familiar about this debate. If you substitute the word 'Microsoft' for 'commercial VLEs' then many of the arguments sound similar to those we have heard regarding a number of Microsoft products, principally the Windows operating system, but also tools such as Word, Excel and server technologies such as Windows NT. The argument is actually about any large corporation with proprietary software, but it is best embodied in the debate around Microsoft. The similarity with VLEs is strengthened when one considers that Microsoft have recently bought a large stake in the company providing the commercial VLE, Blackboard, and that in 2005 Blackboard acquired the other main VLE company, WebCT. This makes the scenario of a 'Microsoft' for educational software, i.e. a very powerful provider who has a near-monopoly, all the more likely.

Windows may have been inferior to the Apple operating system in the early 1990s, and for many software enthusiasts any graphical user interface (GUI) is inferior to a command driven one. Microsoft's success is often portrayed as a result of ruthless business practices and good luck, both of which have indeed played their part. But their success also lies in a willingness to be doggedly pragmatic – they may not offer the best solution, but they offer the most democratic one.

The anti-Microsoft arguments can be classified along three lines:

- The argument from technology – the products are technically inferior to those produced by other means, particularly an open source approach. As software becomes ever more complex, then the best way to create robust, powerful systems is through a distributed approach, rather than a central team. This is captured by the quote from the open source guru Eric Raymond, that 'given enough eyeballs all bugs are shallow'. Just as significantly, proprietary software is often closed, you have to wait for the next release and cannot modify the code yourself. An open source approach allows greater flexibility and adaptability, although it does require a considerable level of expertise to realize this. The open source debate is increasingly important in the VLE field, and we will look at in detail in Chapter 9.
- The argument from economics – there are two elements to this. Firstly, as well as being technically inferior, the centralized mode of production is not an economically viable method of creating software, and a more distributed and open approach is more appropriate. The second element is concerned with the consumer, whereby allowing one producer to become dominant ties them in with one vendor. Given the significance of ICT systems in nearly all organizations, this gives the vendor an enormous influence and locks the customer in to expensive updates and support. It therefore makes financial sense to adopt either a solution that spreads the reliance across vendors or is based around an open source model that is owned by a community.
- The argument from ideology – there is often an evangelizing note to many of the anti-Microsoft arguments, and increasingly it is seen as a

social imperative to deny this level of power and influence to any one institution. This is the OS developer and spokesman, Andreas Pour (Butler 2002):

> We are steadily heading to a future in which the control of humanity's intellectual property – works of art, multimedia, ideas, writings, etc. – is so vested in software vendor(s) that it is fair to say that the average user of a proprietary desktop will eventually no longer 'own', in the traditional sense of the word, his or her own electronic creations. In other words, the products of our creative minds, the very essence of our humanity, are being relentlessly stripped from us.
>
> If you use a proprietary OS to make a video or audio track, or to write a research paper, and save it in one of the default proprietary electronic data formats, you might soon find yourself actually paying someone else run-time and/or license renewal fees *just to access your own creations*. Not to mention any charges that may apply to distributing copies to others (whether directly or because the recipient must also pay similar runtime or recurring fees to access the data). You tell me, when you have to pay one particular vendor money every time you or someone else views a movie you created, who owns the movie?

As with the complaints against the more popular VLE products, it is easy to have sympathy with many of these claims. But that is to miss the point about the function and audience of such software. It is not aimed at the sort of people who raise these objections, but rather at the audience who does not know, and does not care to know, how software works. They just want it to work.

If we return to our normal distribution curve, the point at which Greller suggests the institutional practices start operating represents the point at which the technology moves into the mainstream and this also represents the fault line between two audiences who we can label 'revolutionaries' and 'democrats' (see Figure 2.3). These are analogous to von Hippel's lead and conventional users. In effect these two camps want different things from the technology, and have different priorities, yet around this cross-over point they are forced to coexist on the same system.

There exists a tension between these two audiences at this point, as it represents the moment a new technology moves in to the mainstream. For the revolutionaries this may result in a loss of control, and also represents the point at which the technology itself ceases to be interesting. For the democrats it is the point at which the technology really needs to start performing robustly and for a non-specialized audience.

The products that serve the majority of any audience that reside in the middle part of the normal distribution curve are almost, by definition, not the sort of tools that those who occupy the leading edge find interesting and suitable.

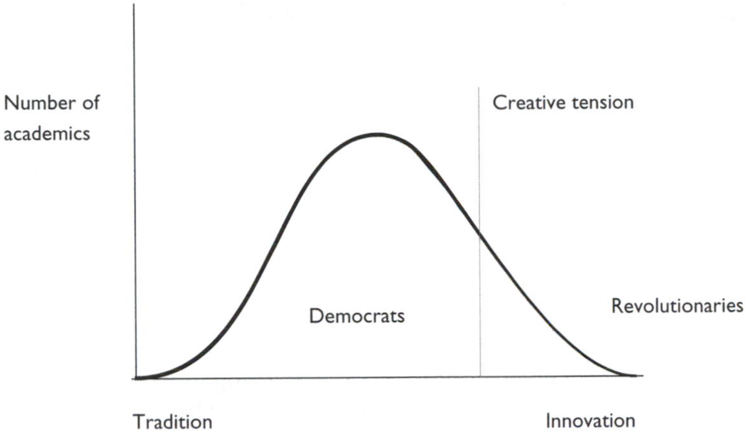

Figure 2.3 'Democrats' and 'revolutionaries' on the normal distribution curve.

The key accusation levelled against such products is their lack of flexibility. But flexibility often arises from a deep understanding of how such tools operate, and what they can be extended to do. This level of complexity is unsuitable for the more pragmatic user. And such flexibility often leads to instability in the hands of the less knowledgeable.

For the revolutionaries it is flexibility, richness, and a strong theoretical underpinning that is important. In short, they like technology that is new and exciting. For the democrats it is robustness, ease of use and practicality that is paramount. These people are concerned with delivery and solving real problems. There is no way around this conflict, and nor should there be, it is a creative tension that is immensely beneficial to both parties, even though they may not recognize it. The revolutionaries will continually push the development of the tools so that they improve, and offer better functionality. The democrats in turn place continual demands on the researchers and developers to create solutions that are actually workable, and not just interesting from a research perspective.

We need to recognize, though, that when we are dealing with any technology these tensions are in place, and this is particularly evident in the debate about VLE options.

In the next two chapters we will look at VLEs from the perspective of both these groups. For the democrats the issue is how to work effectively with the available technologies, while for the revolutionaries it is about the potential of new technologies.

Chapter 3

Using common VLE tools

A VLE can be viewed as a useful collection of e-learning tools in a package that allows a common interface and sharing of data between the tools. While the specifics of any one VLE will vary, on the whole they offer similar functionality. We can think of a VLE as having three dimensions to its functionality, each of which represents a different interface and audience (Figure 3.1). The three dimensions are:

- Institutional – a VLE needs to integrate with other university systems, including student records, library systems, content management, etc. Being able to do this in an efficient manner is a primary concern for the IT specialists who will deploy and support a VLE.
- Academic – although one thinks of students as the end users of a VLE, it is the academic staff who will ultimately determine the success of a VLE. Therefore the methods for creating courses, setting up tools and supporting students will be the key determinants in the popularity of a VLE. Support for a range of subject areas and pedagogies will be important to these users, as well as ease of use.
- Learner – the end user of a VLE can be seen as the learner. If their experience is not a good one, for example the system is difficult to navigate or is not robust, then the feedback and use of the system will be poor, which will inhibit its uptake. For this group the system must be easy to use and consistent in its layout, but most importantly it needs to add value to the learning experience. This is particularly the case when a VLE is deployed on campus. If the system does not add any value, then, being a strategic group, most learners will avoid it. Adding value can be in terms of additional content, more flexible study patterns, increased support and, for some users, a more appropriate environment.

Viewing a VLE as having these three dimensions emphasizes that it is a system that needs to appeal to different audiences, each of whom will have different priorities and needs. A'Herran (2000) suggests that there are four perspectives from which a VLE is analyzed:

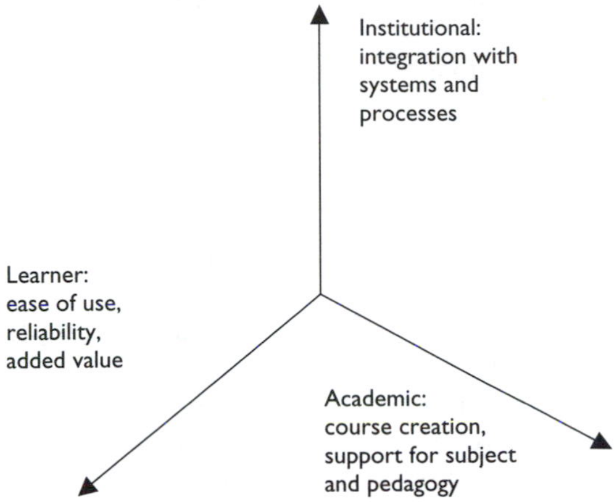

Figure 3.1 The dimensions of a VLE interface.

- Administrators – scalability, value for money and integration with existing systems are important for these users.
- Technicians – robustness, user base, technical support and ease of maintenance will be significant.
- Course developers or teachers – customizability, flexibility and the integration of legacy materials will be paramount.
- Learners – consistency, accessibility and quality of design will be the main concerns.

If we consider the tools that comprise a VLE, then the institutional dimension is the one that stands apart from the others. This will be concerned with populating courses with the appropriate students, allocating the correct roles to students, academics and administrators, recording any assessment and accessing resources. The exact approaches for realizing these tasks will vary according to each VLE. It is worth noting that these can often be a significant factor in determining the choice of VLE, particularly if the choice is being made by a central IT department. The ability for any given VLE to interface with their chosen database technology and to run on their existing configuration will be an influential factor. One should not underestimate the significance that such factors play in successfully deploying a VLE. If many VLEs are similar in terms of their end user functionality, then the ease with which they can be deployed and supported by IT staff and their existing knowledge base is a reasonable deciding factor.

But these are often highly technical and specialized requirements, so for our purposes let us assume that the VLE can interface successfully with existing university systems, and turn our attention to the other two main dimensions, those of academic and learner. These have a high degree of overlap, obviously, with the academic interface often being an extension of that offered to the learner.

The main learning and teaching functions can be summarized as:

- Content delivery – easy upload and management of content in a variety of formats.
- Asynchronous discussion – text based discussion boards that can be easily created and are straightforward to use, with threading of messages and attachment capability.
- Online assessment – a range of assessment tools including multiple choice, matching pairs and short text answers.
- Student tracking – the ability to record a student's progress through a course and have this information presented in a concise format.
- Synchronous discussion – text based discussion in real time, perhaps combined with other real time tools such as a shared whiteboard or webcasting.
- Student tools – these usually include a calendar, a personal area for uploading resources, a note-taking tool, and email.

This is a bare-bones list of the functionality VLEs provide. Within each function there will be additional capability depending on the particular VLE, for instance some asynchronous discussion tools can show the history of who has read a message, have the ability to quote previous messages, allow the user to change the view of the messages, provide summarizing tools, can be embedded within content, etc. While the basic list above can certainly be improved upon, it still represents a comprehensive set of tools with which a great deal can be achieved pedagogically. Ten years ago having such a tool -set freely available would have seemed an embarrassment of riches, and so we should not underestimate what can be achieved with this standard functionality.

There are two points that I would wish to make about existing VLE tools, when they are implemented out of the box:

1. They are good enough, if not ideal, for most teaching approaches. We are not waiting for a new technology to implement effective e-learning, just the imaginative application of existing tools.
2. The more basic the tool, the greater the onus is on the educator to coordinate, facilitate and organize the activity. There is a general migration of this coordination role to software systems as they develop. However, even more complex online activities can be achieved with basic tools if they are facilitated appropriately.

Armed with these two precepts we can now look at what can be achieved with existing tools.

Pedagogies and e-learning

In order to think about how VLEs can support e-learning, it is first necessary to consider the various teaching approaches that you might want to realize online. Below are eight pedagogical approaches which cover a broad spectrum of the type of learning experience delivered online (however, none of these approaches is exclusive to e-learning, they are equally applicable in a face-to-face context). We will revisit these pedagogies when we look at other tools that can be deployed within a VLE. The pedagogies are:

- community of practice/socio-cultural learning;
- resource-based learning;
- peer learning;
- content-led/instructivist learning;
- complex learning;
- problem-based learning;
- collaborative learning;
- instructor-led learning.

Before we look at each of these it is worth noting that, although it is undeniably important, pedagogy is not the sole factor in determining a course design. Other factors will include the available finances, time and resources, as well as the intended audience and programme context of a course. Each of these would provide a different perspective for a course and often an educator has to balance all of these considerations. So, it is rarely a matter of simply deciding 'which is the best way to teach this subject?' but rather deciding the best way to teach this subject for the audience in question, with the staff available, the budget allocation and the time frame set by operational requirements.

The approaches detailed below should not be viewed as mutually exclusive. There is a good deal of overlap between many of them and often it is a matter of emphasis. It is also likely that no single approach would be used in a course to the exclusion of all others, and a mix of one or more approaches is common. However, it is useful to separate them out for the purpose of thinking about how VLEs can be used to support and realize the particular demands of such an approach.

Community of practice/socio-cultural learning

This approach is based around the principles of engagement, intelligibility and participation. It assumes that learning is a social process and that an academic discipline represents a community, to which the student is enculturated.

Resource-based learning

If one views the internet as a vast collection of resources, then it naturally lends itself to an approach which encourages students to use a variety of resources to develop their understanding, rather than a specified few provided by the educator. Being able to analyse, select and critique resources is a major educational benefit. Such an approach may be realized through the creation of one or more activities, which students perform as individuals or in groups, in which they must solve a problem or produce an output by working with a range of resources. This is the type of approach that has been greatly enhanced by the internet as it gives unparalleled access to a wide range of resources. As it is not about the transmission of predetermined content, nor solely about discussion, this is an example of an approach that blends both the discussion and the broadcast viewpoints.

Peer learning

In this approach learning is viewed as a social construct which is largely achieved by peer-to-peer interaction. There is a strong emphasis on interacting with and learning from peers. Students share and comment upon each other's material. This is related to the communities of practice approach, although it is arguable that in a community of practice, a hierarchy, or degrees of membership, exist whereas peer learning views all individuals on the same level. It is also possible to implement peer, or collaborative, learning without necessarily adopting a socio-cultural perspective to learning.

Content-led/instructivist learning

This approach focuses mainly on content (which can be related to the subject matter or developing general skills), with little focus on explicit, peer-to-peer communication (although one could argue that all courses are the result of discussion within the course team and the student learns through dialogue with the material). The emphasis is largely on individuals interacting with that content.

Complex learning

This approach focuses on the type of learning that takes place across or between courses. It is concerned with the development of complex skills such as critical thinking, analysis, synthesis and evaluation as well as metacognitive skills. These go beyond an appreciation of the particular subject matter and require considerable time to develop (5,000 hours has been suggested). They are also the type of skills that employers frequently say they require of graduates.

Problem-based learning

In this approach students are given an 'ill-structured problem', that is a problem or scenario about which they do not currently possess enough information to reach a solution. This then requires them to find the appropriate information and to gain any skills necessary to solve the problem.

Collaborative learning

One of the main advantages of the internet for distance educators is that it allows collaboration and cooperation among students. A course that uses this pedagogy will base much of the activity around group tasks and discussion. Collaborative tasks can include students working towards a joint goal, for instance constructing a group document or website. There is also a focus on discussion, so online debates may be adopted.

Instructor-led learning

This may also be termed an information-transfer, didactic or instructivist model. In this approach the educator or instructor imparts knowledge to the students. This is the traditional mode of education, as embodied in the lecture.

E-learning with common VLE tools

If we now return to our basic set of VLE tools, we can look at each of the pedagogies outlined in the previous section and consider how they can be realized in an e-learning context, using the common set of tools.

Community of practice/socio-cultural learning

Given the social dimension to this approach, the discussion boards will play a central role. The central tenet of this approach is that students are brought into a culture, in this case that of the academic discipline they are studying. That culture has its own accepted practice, standard knowledge, mores and values. Therefore it is not just engagement with peers that is important, but also observation and interaction with established community members. Thus webcasts and guest lectures can play an important role, in allowing students to interact with other experts, and to feel part of the community they are migrating into.

Exposure to a range of resources is also necessary to ensure that students are enculturated into both the mode of expression in the community and the main areas of debate. Thus a well-populated resource area and library linkage would be suitable. In some subject areas where there is a strong practical element, then video clips will be beneficial. Audio and video will be more important with this approach than some others, as it aids students' engagement with the community if they can see and/or hear interviews, demonstrations, or lectures from the main personalities. A good deal of the focus for this approach and, by implication, the effort of the educator, will be in supporting analysis, discussion and critical engagement with the resources, as this will tease out the misconceptions and build a consensus of understanding. In this approach engagement with the broader community may also be important, for example student nurses interacting with practising nurses, computer science students engaging with professional programmers. This can easily be realized by monitoring or participating in discussion lists, newsgroups or forums found on the internet. These can be integrated within the VLE or portal as part of a news feed (see Chapter 6).

Assessment for a course with this philosophy is likely to be based around a real, or at least pseudo-real, problem, such as might be encountered in the community itself. As such, independent or group research is liable to play a significant role in the assessment activity. If this is the case then access to a rich set of resources will be necessary – these can be housed within the VLE, or through access to another system, such as a content management or library system. Here the institutional dimension of the VLE is significant in allowing seamless integration with other systems. Another feature that may be important is a personal storage area for each student. Most VLEs have such a facility, which can vary in sophistication, ranging from a straightforward 'dumping' area for any resources to more structured tools that allow descriptions to be added to resources and for them to be organized in an e-portfolio (we will look at e-portfolios in more detail in the next chapter).

Resource-based learning

To support this pedagogy would require the use of a threaded discussion board in the VLE, since this approach places a strong emphasis on the interpretation of a vast range of resources, so support and dialogue between peers and the educator is vital. This approach will also require sophisticated library access and search tools. Perhaps more than any other approach, this will require students to go outside the confines of the VLE, and seek out resources elsewhere. However, if they are not to spend all their time searching, then the integration of databases, repositories and resource banks in to the VLE will be necessary. The degree of integration will vary, from simply providing a link, to more sophisticated federated search tools that can search across a range of databases and return results. Federated search is an area that is more dependent on the uptake of standards (both technical and descriptive) than it is on the development of a particular technology. We will return to this later when we consider the relationship between the VLE and library systems.

Increasingly VLEs are being used as content management systems themselves. While they may not have some of the sophistication of a dedicated CMS, they have the benefit of being the tool that academics are familiar with.

There is also a motivation for academics to upload material, as they are doing so to create a specific course for specific students. The benefits of a dedicated CMS, which promises future reuse, sophisticated management, tagging and description of resources and standards compliance may seem somewhat ephemeral when a deadline looms. Thus a VLE represents a reasonable compromise for many institutions, and as VLE manufacturers realize this, the CMS capability is being promoted and developed. A VLE configured to offer a CMS function represents a resource base for students on other, similar courses, even if the resources are often limited to the specific institution or faculty.

Other common VLE tools which would be useful in such an approach include an online note-taking tool and the personal area for organizing resources mentioned above. As much of the content in such a scenario would be external to the institution, there is a need to ensure students are gaining an appropriate understanding of the topic. Much of this will be done through formal assessment and dialogue, but there would also be a need for additional aids for the student to test their learning, for example a range of formative quizzes and tests. Many VLEs have the ability to selectively release material, so there can be inbuilt checks in a system; for example, if a student scores badly on a particular test then specific resources that have been pre-selected can be made available, thus ensuring all students are on track. Similarly tools that aid the educator in guiding students through activities with such broad boundaries will be necessary. These could include feedback from student tracking, so student progress can be monitored, as well as support tools such as synchronous discussion, so that regular online 'drop in' sessions can be conducted.

Peer learning

For peer learning to be effective communication tools need to be at the fore. This will usually be in the form of asynchronous discussion boards. There will be a demand on the educator to structure these, for example so that each group or topic has its own discussion area, and to monitor and facilitate the discussion. Synchronous tools that allow real-time group meetings will also be required to facilitate debate, organize tasks, share ideas and so on. The standard tools will be adequate for much of this, although an instant messaging tool that notifies users when others are online may also be beneficial in establishing ongoing and impromptu dialogue.

Sharing resources is also a key component in this approach. This can be achieved through discussion boards and the use of attachments to messages, although this is not the most elegant solution. Many VLEs have the capacity for shared group areas, similar to the personal areas, where groups of students can upload content for others to view. These can be associated with other tools, for example shared whiteboards. Such an area will need to support content in a range of media.

Less common in the standard VLEs is an inbuilt peer assessment tool that supports the random allocation of a marker to each assignment. Some VLEs have this capacity as an extension to their more standard assignment handling provision, but the same result can be achieved through the use of discussion boards or email, although this places the emphasis on the educator to allocate markers and coordinate the process. As such it is an example of the second principle set out in this chapter, in that the educator has to accommodate much of the effort that a specialized tool would otherwise absorb.

Content-led/instructivist learning

This can be viewed as the standard mode for most VLEs, so it is the one to which they are best suited. Key to this is the ease of use of the academic interface, as it encourages educators to upload and organize content. Most VLEs support a wide range of formats, including animation, text, images, video and audio, so content can be rich and varied, without an over-emphasis on text. If the main focus is on content then there is an onus on that content to carry some of the interaction necessary for effective learning, whereas in many of the other approaches this interaction component is satisfied through dialogue and collaboration. Interactive content can be achieved through animations (for example Flash) and simulations, which most VLEs will import as content. However, the system is usually ignorant of what happens within these interactive elements; it simply acts as a holding place for them. If there is little integration between the content and the VLE then this will have a negative effect on other functions that rely on the exchange of data, for example student tracking. There is then a role for informal assessment to play in testing the understanding gained through such applications, and so extensive use of a variety of online testing tools will be required.

Standard discussion boards are adequate for this approach, as they play a more peripheral role than seen in some other approaches. Depending on the subject area, mathematical or scientific notation can be problematic for some VLEs to deal with, for example when creating online tests, and often the solution is to resort to images of equations, which severely restricts some of their potential.

Complex learning

Complex learning, which typically occurs at the programme level, that is across individual modules or courses, reveals some of the limitations of current VLEs. The typical unit of currency for VLEs is the individual module or course (for example introductory mathematics), rather than the programme level (for example a computer science degree). This is a function of the focus on the academic dimension. In order for VLEs to be accepted and used by educators this interface is aimed at the individual educator, or small team, creating their specific course online. Thus, although there may be templates which define a common approach and look and feel for courses within a particular programme, most VLEs are designed around the notion of the course, with the structure, administration and support tools matched suitably. For example, tools such as discussion boards, email and calendars are set up so that the students on a particular course can access them, but mixing access with a wider group can be problematic.

Thus creating space for learning to occur across, between and after specific courses can prove difficult. It can be managed but the solutions sometimes seem unwieldy, for example creating a separate 'course' which constitutes the programme. A VLE needs to have a strong organizational role in this type of learning, providing a portfolio area for students to collect information, evidence, and an online diary (blog) to promote reflection and ongoing activity. An online note-taking tool and a means of organizing references would also be required. These tools are offered by some VLEs, but are by no means standard, although simple integration with third party tools, for example a commercial blogging tool, would not be problematic.

Complex learning is an approach where the use of a student portal would also be important. Portals can be used to provide information at an institutional level, and can also be customized so that individuals receive information appropriate to them. We will look at portals in more detail later. The portal embodies the individual's relationship with the institution, but often this is realized in terms of information feeds – for example, students studying for an MBA will get university news relevant to business students and perhaps also feeds from the *Financial Times* and *Wall Street Journal*. Increasingly, however, the portal is seen as the area where a number of personal tools should properly reside, for example an e-portfolio, blog, organizer, etc. These are tools which can also be found or incorporated into a VLE. This demonstrates two things, first that there is a tension between VLEs and portals as to where services and information should best be positioned, and second, that increasingly VLEs are seen as a collection of services, which can be decoupled and made available in multiple interfaces. We will explore this tension in more detail in Chapter 6.

Some VLEs are packaged with a portal, and others have some inbuilt portal functionality. This is important in the context of complex learning as there is a need for both personalized and customized information feeds to students and alumni highlighting news and events related to their subject area as well as programme-relevant news. The calendar and organizer tool that can be populated automatically from different data sources will also prove beneficial. With much talk and emphasis on 'communities of practice' a programme- or community-wide discussion board will be a useful means of helping students match theory to practice and to see common themes between individual courses. Use of synchronous tools, particularly webcasting, would be required, to convey programme-wide events such as expert lectures or day-schools.

Problem-based learning

Problem-based learning is often, but not necessarily, collaborative in nature, so the collaborative tools will be required, including synchronous and asynchronous communication tools. Tools which aid document sharing and collaboration will also be necessary for the groups, and as with peer learning this can be accomplished through the use of shared workspaces or the use of attachments in discussion boards.

In this approach students are usually given a real-world task and by using a number of resources they are expected to gain the necessary knowledge required to complete it. Thus, as with some previous approaches, access to a range of well-structured resources will be important. Unlike resource-based learning there will be less emphasis on discovering the resource and so the standard means of presenting and organizing content in VLEs will suffice.

The role of the educator in such an approach is a difficult one, as they often have to manage separate groups, where much of the activity occurs 'out of sight'. Therefore system level aids are beneficial. These would include system generated reports based on student tracking data. Extensive use of formative assessment tools would also be useful, for students to gauge their own understanding.

Collaborative learning

For collaborative learning the accent is on dialogue and communication. Asynchronous discussion tools will be important here, and the students would benefit from them being more sophisticated than the more basic tools, so for example they can see who has read messages, can easily reference other messages by linking, can add attachments in different formats and can summarize threads. There are 'manual' means of achieving some of these (for example referencing a message by its name) but the approach can be facilitated by some of the better discussion tools currently available.

A range of synchronous collaborative tools may also be useful, including shared whiteboards, audio-conferencing, chat rooms and instant messaging. These are often combined in a single tool embedded within a VLE, although such a tool is often simply called from within the VLE, but the rest of the system remains essentially dumb to what occurs within the synchronous tools. This means that capturing or recording the output or tracking activity within it can be difficult.

As much of this approach is focused around discussion it highlights one weakness with many current VLEs, and that is the disjuncture between content and dialogue. The common practice is to have content presented with discussion boards listed separately. Thus you can read some text, and then go to a discussion board, but the two are not combined in any direct way. While this is appropriate for general discussion, it is sometimes desirable to have the discussion embedded within the content so that dialogue can proceed from a particular point and at the time it is required.

Instructor-led learning

As with content-led, this can be seen as the approach that current VLEs most readily support. Much of the focus of development of current VLEs has gone into the academic dimension so that they are easy to use, both conceptually and technically. Thus they readily support the pedagogic practice academics are most familiar with, namely the lecture. It is easy to structure a course in folders, populate these with lecture notes and presentations, and create a discussion forum alongside, and this gives a simple replication of a standard course. Indeed this is one of the common criticisms of VLEs, particularly from the revolutionaries, in that they encourage this mode of operation, which ensures that the e-learning alternative is usually a poor substitute for face-to-face education, and also educators do not engage with the new demands and possibilities of the medium. While there is some truth in these accusations, this low-friction approach for academics has also been the reason behind the substantial growth in the VLE market. It has also returned some of the democratization and liberation found in the first generation of e-learning. I have argued elsewhere (Weller 2002) that one of the initial attractions of using the internet as an educational tool was that the educator was brought in to close proximity with the finished product. In the early stages of e-learning this was realized through the creation of simple websites. These were an order of magnitude easier to create than, say, a multimedia CD-ROM, which usually required professional programmers and designers, who essentially came between the academic and the finished product. The ability to create your own website and add in discussion tools was quite liberating for many academics. However, as tastes became more sophisticated the product that a sole, 'amateur' web designing academic could achieve was not adequate, and so the professional programmers moved back in, re-establishing that distance from the finished product. VLEs return some of this power to academics so that they can create, structure, experiment and engage with the technology on their own terms, although the degree to which they have power will be determined by their institution's IT policies.

Conclusion

In this chapter we have looked at a number of pedagogical approaches, and seen how these can be supported by standard VLE tools currently available. Some approaches are supported more easily than others, and some require a good deal of intervention in order to realize them within the limitations of the tools. However, this range of approaches (and many more not mentioned here) *can* be achieved in current VLEs, and often by an educator without the need for specialist technical support, or a great deal of technical knowledge. This is the position of the democrats, that VLE tools are robust, easy to use and broad enough to meet most needs.

In the next chapter we will turn to newer technologies more favoured by the revolutionaries, and taking the same pedagogical approaches see how these can be supported.

Chapter 4

Beyond the VLE

In this chapter we will look at a number of newer technologies and see how these can be used to realize the pedagogies outlined in the previous chapter. Looking at technologies is always a moving target, and at the time of writing some of these, blogs for example, are already seen as part of the mainstream. As such they may become integrated within a VLE and form part of the standard tool set. Here they will become more of interest to democrats, and less so to revolutionaries who will be looking at new technologies.

The technologies we will consider in this chapter are:

- blogs;
- wikis;
- podcasting;
- social software;
- structured conferencing;
- instant messaging;
- e-portfolios.

These are outlined below.

Blogs

Web logs, or blogs, have become the fastest growing use of the internet over recent years. Blood (2000) differentiates between two types of blog: the journal and the filter. The journal acts as an online diary and contains thoughts, opinions, reflections, etc. This is usually personal, giving an account of the individual's life. The second type is the filter-style blog, where the blogger posts links to other web content (be it obscure or mainstream), with a commentary on this. This second type is probably of more interest and value to the reader. As Blood (2000) puts it:

> A filter-style weblog provides many advantages to its readers. It reveals glimpses of an unimagined web to those who have no time to surf.

> An intelligent human being filters through the mass of information packaged daily for our consumption and picks out the interesting, the important, the overlooked, and the unexpected. This human being may provide additional information to that which corporate media provides, expose the fallacy of an argument, perhaps reveal an inaccurate detail. Because the weblog editor can comment freely on what she finds, one week of reading will reveal to you her personal biases, making her a predictable source. This further enables us to turn a critical eye to both the information and comments she provides. Her irreverent attitude challenges the veracity of the 'facts' presented each day by authorities.

In June 2003 Blogcount.com estimated there were approximately 2.9 million active blogs and by January 2005 there were reportedly 20 million in South Korea alone (Brake 2005). This demonstrates the rate of growth of blogging, although these figures are difficult to verify, particularly if one makes a distinction between 'active' bloggers and those who happen to be given blogging functionality as part of a general internet provision. Indeed blogging's uptake has been so rapid that it could already be considered mainstream, with 70 per cent of respondents to a US survey aware of blogs (although only 30 per cent had visited one), and 52 per cent supporting the same rights for bloggers as journalists (LeMay 2005).

The development of easy to use tools such as Blogger.com, Radio Userland and MoveableType has meant that users can easily publish diaries from any location. They can allow comments on each of their postings, thus creating debate around issues of importance to a particular set of individuals. Communities of bloggers have grown up, linking and commenting on each other's postings. There are also community blogs, such as MetaFilter, which anyone can post to and discuss issues on.

Blogs are a technologically simple development, yet they have been seized upon by the internet community for a number of reasons. First, they greatly increase the degree of openness by allowing simple 'push-button' publishing. There is no need to design and upload web pages – the user can choose from a variety of design templates, and then simply type their text in to a box and click on publish. Second, they take advantage of the internet's global pervasiveness so people can update from anywhere. So, for example, many people keep blogs as they undertake their world trip. For others they form part of the commentary and knowledge sharing within a community. For example, Lisa Guernsey (2003) gives this example:

> Some people who have experienced the phenomenon cite a speech given last year at a computer industry conference by Joe Nacchio, former chief executive of the telecommunications company Qwest. As he gave his presentation, two bloggers – Dan Gillmor, a columnist for *The San Jose Mercury News*, and Doc Searls, senior editor for *The Linux Journal* –

> were posting notes about him to their Weblogs, which were simultaneously being read by many people in the audience.
>
> Both included a link forwarded by a reader in Florida to a stock filing report indicating that Mr. Nacchio had recently made millions of dollars from selling his company's stock, although he complained in his speech about the tough economy.
>
> 'No sympathy here,' Mr. Gillmor wrote.
>
> 'When Dan blogged that, the tenor of the room changed,' Mr. Doctorow said. Mr. Nacchio, he said, 'stopped getting softball questions and he started getting hardball questions.'

In addition, blogs have become a useful and trusted information source, with much of the informed debate that used to be found in newsgroups now taking place in blogs. As mentioned, bloggers will often post comments on other bloggers' postings, thus creating a distributed debate. Because these are owned by the individual user they are much less susceptible to the kind of attack that has crippled many newsgroups.

Wikis

The online encyclopedia, Wikipedia, defines a wiki as 'a group of Web pages that allows users to add content, as on an Internet forum, but also permits others (often completely unrestricted) to edit the content'. The key point here is that anyone can change the content, unlike most web pages that are static and can only be altered by the originator or those with specific access.

A good example of a wiki is Wikipedia itself. This adopts much the same principle as seen in open source software development, which is that for completing complex projects it is often best to have a wide community to do the work. In the case of open source this allows complex pieces of software (such as the web server software Apache) to be developed by having a large community contribute small changes, run tests, suggest improvements, etc. The same principle applies when creating a large knowledge base such as an encyclopedia. Wikipedia gets around this by allowing everyone to contribute. Thus you can alter a definition if you want to, or if one does not exist you can create a new entry.

Podcasting

Podcasting can be seen as a logical extension to blogs. In some respects they can be viewed as audio blogs. It is also a type of low resource radio broadcast. The technology is again relatively simple (hence its popularity). Users create and upload audio files to a website or server, usually in MP3 format. These can be downloaded by other users and, because they are in the appropriate format, they can be played on portable audio devices such as Apple's iPod (hence the name). You can just as easily play the files on your computer; podcasting doesn't require an iPod. The other important feature of podcasting is the ability to be syndicated in the same way that blogs can, using a protocol known as RSS (Really Simple Syndication, or Rich Site Summary). This allows users to create lists of blogs or podcasts which they wish to be kept up to date with, and the software will automatically search for any additions to these feeds and download them, thus saving the user the effort of continually trawling across different providers. This ability to automatically update makes podcasting an ideal technology for regular or sporadic broadcasts, which can be personal reflections, amateur radio shows, news or lectures.

In 2005 Stanford University teamed up with Apple's iTunes (http://itunes.stanford.edu/) to distribute audio files of lectures and interviews, thus allowing students, alumni and anyone with an interest to listen to this content in a convenient format, and to subscribe so they could receive regular updates. This is not intended to replace standard lectures but rather represents an alternative means of distributing information and particularly of keeping alumni connected to the university.

Structured conferencing

Asynchronous text-based communication systems are now in widespread use in e-learning and, apart from content delivery, are the most important and popular tool within VLEs, to the extent that we almost take them for granted and don't question how they function. The use of such systems for collaborative activity probably represents the most abundant area in e-learning publications and research. There exist a number of practical guides and advice for the educator in structuring such activity (for example Salmon 2004, McConnell 1994).

While asynchronous communication has proven immensely popular and successful in education there are often problems with online activities and discussions, which need careful management, including lack of participation, resistance to participation, unfocused discussion, fractured discussion that is difficult to follow, manipulation by the strongest member and so on.

Most of the research and literature is based around similar technology and focuses on the educator's role in establishing, facilitating and coordinating activity. Some researchers have begun to examine the manner in which computer mediated environments influence communication, and to design environments to specifically encourage certain types of interaction, and we will look at this in a later chapter when we examine the concept of affordances.

By implementing different types of control, functionality and interface, it is possible to subtly alter the way in which these tools are used, and the type of communication that occurs within them. One such example is the H20 project at Harvard University which aims to develop software based around strong pedagogical principles. The first release of such software is the Rotisserie system. This is a structured conferencing system that seeks to overcome some of the problems often found in online discussion by introducing an element of organization and compulsion. The Rotisserie website claims:

> The Rotisserie implements an innovative approach to online discussion that encourages measured, thoughtful discourse in a way that traditional threaded messaging systems cannot. In contrast to the completely asynchronous, broadcast-to-broadcast mode of existing threaded messaging systems, the Rotisserie adds structure to both the timing and the flow of the discussion.
>
> (http://h2oproject.law.harvard.edu/rotisserie.html)

Rotisserie is based around a series of rounds, so that all users who are signed up for a Rotisserie session will be sent an email, telling them to respond to an original posting by a set deadline. They may post their reply at any time prior to this deadline, but it is not published until the deadline has passed. In the next round, each member is assigned (randomly or according to set rules) another posting to respond to, again within a set timeframe, and so on, depending on how many rounds the educator has determined. This allows for far more structured and controlled dialogue.

Such a system may not be suitable for all forms of dialogue, for example Wegerif (1998) argues that the social dimension of CMC plays an important role and this system does not allow for 'frivolous' or off-topic postings. However, it can be used for specific tasks, for instance it can be used to set up time-limited discussions around specific resources or questions, or it can be used as a peer assessment system, with each student being randomly assigned another's submission to mark. As such it is a good example of how an existing technology can be modified to fulfill a particular function or to facilitate a certain type of behaviour. Rotisserie does this by adding stronger levels of control, whereas wikis can be seen as implementing the opposite in terms of control levels, and passing absolute control over the content to the wider community. Both are valid approaches if you are aware of what they offer and what you want to achieve in a particular activity. We will look at this matching of tool to approach in more detail when we consider affordances in a later chapter.

Instant messaging

Instant messaging (IM) is, as its name suggests, a means of communicating in real time via the internet. Rather like blogging its use is so widespread now that it can be thought of as a mainstream technology, although its use in a formal education context is still limited. It is achieved by means of a software client, for example AOL's Instant Messenger. Users who all have the same client can create a list of people with whom they wish to communicate. The IM client will notify the user when these people come online. Users can set their status to indicate whether they are busy, away or so forth, so other users know whether to contact them. It has the advantage over email in that you can be certain the recipient has read your message. The synchronous nature of the communication also has a number of advantages (and disadvantages).

Just as asynchronous email changed the nature of communication, so IM has had an effect on the type of communication people engage in and their online behaviour. In many ways, as email has moved into the mainstream of communication within organizations, IM has become the means by which much informal, social interaction takes place.

A Pew Internet report (2001) talks of an instant messaging generation, with 74 per cent of online teens using IM. Although it has long been popular with teenagers, it has recently penetrated the workplace and been formally adopted by some organizations, such as IBM (Dean 2000). IM is used for informal discussion, often of a social nature. This can have implications in education, as Nicholson (2002) reports, where students who used IM reported a stronger sense of community and found it easier to communicate.

IM represents one of the technologies, along with PDAs (personal digital assistants) and mobile phones that students will bring with them to their higher education experience, regardless of whether it is formally incorporated into that learning experience. Having an appreciation of the type of communication it supports is therefore important in understanding the broader context in which a student is operating.

Social software

The term social software has gained much currency since 2002 and is usually attributed to Clay Shirky, who organized a social software summit in that year. It can be seen as a catch-all for a number of software developments that have taken place independently. Social software can be defined as software that promotes interactions in groups and the formation of community. Established internet technologies such as discussion boards and email even could be termed social software, although it is generally used to refer to more recent technologies. Blogs, wikis and instant messaging could certainly be subsumed under the term social software, but I have deliberately separated them out here as they have gained sufficient identities of their own. Like many terms it is both useful, and almost superfluous. Given that the internet fosters dialogue and communication, one's reaction to the development of social software could be, 'Well of *course* there's social software, that's what the net is for.'

What has been interesting recently is the number of tools that have relatively low threshold, in terms of user time and effort, for joining and participating.

One of the prohibitive factors of intensive social tools (such as instant messaging) is that they require a good deal of time investment in order to gain benefit from them. This is why they often seem to appeal to teenagers who have the requisite time to talk, and aren't spending it, say, commuting, or caring for children. However, a number of new tools have taken advantage of the size of communities to offer low threshold but rewarding experiences. For instance the site Flickr allows users to upload pictures, tag these with fairly easy data, add commentaries and share them. There is nothing particularly new or sophisticated about this from a technological perspective, but it takes advantage of three trends – one is the pervasiveness of digital cameras, the second is the proliferation of broadband so that uploading large image files is now feasible for most users and the third is the general level of familiarity and comfort most users have with internet technologies now. These factors combined with a good site and word of mouth recommendation has made Flickr something of a phenomenon as people share images, search for similar ones, and then blog about images they find, and so on.

Similarly 43things has lists of things people want to do ranging from the innocuous ('drink more tea') to the bizarre ('learn how to tie the stem of a maraschino cherry with my tongue'). The number and location of users wanting to do the same thing is displayed. Users can share ideas, see who else wants to do the same things, provide feedback if they have done the task in question, share images (through Flickr), etc.

Social bookmarking probably has the most ready application to education. Sites such as del.icio.us allow users to share bookmarks they find on the web. This has the benefit of creating clusters of activity around useful sites, and as with lists and recommendations in commercial sites such as Amazon, they allow users to find similar pages. Other applications that might be grouped under social software include virtual worlds, social libraries and social networks.

E-portfolio

E-portfolios have gained a good deal of currency since 2003, although relatively few institutions are using them yet, and even those that are do not exploit the full potential of the technology. Before we look at the various types of e-portfolios, it is worth considering some of the drivers behind the development of e-portfolios. The most significant of these is probably the recognition of, and push for, lifelong learning. To sustain a knowledge economy the workers in that economy need to continually develop new knowledge and skills, thus there is an imperative for many developed countries to promote lifelong learning as a cultural expectation. In such a scenario a learner will move across many different institutions during their lifetime to partake in their education, and also undergo learning in a variety of formats that do not all fit the very formal, examined and accredited model. There is a need therefore for a learning record that is personal to, and owned by, the individual. Related to this is the move towards recognizing informal, or non-formal, learning, such as that gained through experience at work. This is usually realized through competencies, for which the individual needs to provide sufficient evidence. As soon as lifelong learning and competencies become a requirement, then it soon follows that a tool to help individuals plan their learning and actions will also be required.

Meeting these needs provides us with the basic e-portfolio tools. Educause defines an e-portfolio as 'a collection of authentic and diverse evidence, drawn from a larger archive, that represents what a person or organization has learned over time, on which the person or organization has reflected, designed for presentation to one or more audiences for a particular rhetorical purpose'. A recent JISC report (Richardson and Ward 2005) describes them as 'a collection (or archive) of reflective writing and associated evidence, which documents learning and which a learner may draw upon to present her/his learning and achievements'. The key functions of any e-portfolio then are the collection, organization and presentation of various assets, pieces of evidence, commentary, etc.

The IMS e-portfolio specification (IMS 2005a) suggests that the types of information it can contain are:

- about digital and non-digital works created or part-created by the subject;
- about the subject of the e-portfolio;
- about activities in which the subject has participated, is participating, or plans to participate;
- about the competencies (skills, etc.) of the subject;
- about the achievements of the subject, whether or not certificated;
- about the subject's preferences;
- about the subject's goals and plans;
- about the subject's interests and values;
- any notes, reflections or assessments relevant to any other part;
- the results of any test or examination of the subject;
- contextual information to help the interpretation of any results;
- the relationships between the other parts of the information (see elsewhere for discussion);
- about the creation and ownership of the parts of the e-portfolio.

It goes on to provide six categories of e-portfolio:

1. Assessment – used to demonstrate achievement against some criteria.
2. Presentation – used to evidence learning in a persuasive way, often relate to professional qualifications.
3. Learning – used to document, guide and advance learning over time.
4. Personal development – related to professional development and employment.

5 Multiple owner – allow more than one person to participate in development of content.
6 Working – combine previous types, with one or more e-portfolios and also a wider archive.

Unlike the other tools mentioned here, e-portfolios represent much more of a complete system, rather than an additional tool which could be incorporated into a VLE. With the appropriate emphasis one could imagine an e-portfolio becoming the central focus of a student's online experience, and thus supplanting the VLE. Many e-portfolio tools are beginning to incorporate discussion facilities, blog tools, secure data transfer with university systems, automatic testing and so on. Having a multiplicity of these tools will be confusing and students are likely to opt for the ones they find most beneficial, so there may be something of a power struggle to come between VLEs and e-portfolios, and this will reflect a conflict between using the institutional systems (VLEs) and personal systems (e-portfolios, plus other tools the student has accrued, such as their preferred IM client), which we will look at when we consider personal learning environments (PLEs).

E-learning with new tools

If we now return to the pedagogies we looked at in the previous chapter, we can examine how these technologies might be used to realize them.

Community of practice/socio-cultural learning

This approach is particularly well suited to the social aspect inherent in many of the tools presented here. A community of practice could form around a wiki, which is seeded with current documents or code, and which is then altered and improved by contributing individuals. Students can participate or observe this process in action, but significantly they will witness the negotiation of meaning between experts in that field.

Further access to experts and experience of being part of a community could be realized through podcasting and blogs. The informality of these tools makes them more likely to be adopted by experts in a given subject area, thus giving students direct exposure to the main debates and issues. For example, Larry Lessig, one of the recognized experts in internet law and rights keeps a blog (http://www.lessig.org/blog/) which is used as both a source of information and a means to ignite debate by those with an interest in this area.

The use of social software such as bookmarking tools also encourages the sense of belonging to a community. By using the clustering notion behind sites such as 43things, topics of interest within the domain could be created, allowing students to focus on areas of similar interest (for example 'I'm worried about the exam').

All of these tools increase the student's enculturation into a community by increasing their sense of identity with that community and by exposing the key concepts and values that operate within the community.

Resource-based learning

The use of an e-portfolio type tool to facilitate the gathering of resources would be useful, and blogs and podcasts would represent a broader range of resources to draw upon. Perhaps more relevant for this approach would be the social facilitation of the discovery of resources. Thus social tools adapted for educational use, but based upon del.icio.us, Flickr and 43things would facilitate learners in finding similar resources, because the searching capacity of many individuals is combined, and the systems make use of tagging to describe content.

Similarly, social networking tools and some IM clients allow users to create profiles and then to search for people with similar interests (for example, 'I'm looking to chat with someone in Seattle who is interested in flower arranging'). By adapting this profiling facility students could find people with academic interests or resources to share. Peer-to-peer programs (such as Kazaa) that facilitate file sharing could also be used to achieve this, similar to the original version of Napster which allowed users to swap music files.

Peer learning

Peer learning would resemble the previous two approaches but with less emphasis on external resources and experts. Thus wiki versions of content (or even assignments) would be available to students to annotate and amend, they would each maintain blogs and share comments between these. Instant messaging would be well suited to this approach, particularly the buddy alerts, which allow students to engage in discussion with peers when they come online. This facilitates a much more casual type of dialogue, such as is commonly found in social environments on campus universities (bars, cafes), where the majority of peer learning occurs conventionally.

Content-led/instructivist learning

Just as this approach was the one to which standard VLEs were most suited, it is probably the approach to which the newer, more socially oriented tools are least well suited. However, the use of such tools in conjunction with more standard content-based structures can facilitate learning. For example, a wiki version of a course running alongside the conventional one would provide students with a space within which they can question, comment upon or update the content, thus potentially improving it for future cohorts.

Tools which demonstrate clustering could be adapted so that students can see who is studying any one page and, in conjunction with instant messaging, invite students who are looking at that page to discuss it, thus creating a real time, impromptu study group.

Complex learning

Complex learning would most benefit from e-portfolios, indeed a means of gathering resources and monitoring progress is almost a requirement for complex learning to take place. As mentioned in the discussion on e-portfolios it is essential that such a tool resides with the individual, and not the institution, as the individual is likely to interact with multiple institutions.

Complex learning also requires a good deal of reflection, and thus blogs would be an ideal tool to promote a longitudinal view to the learning process. The establishment of a good social network within which connections and experiences can be shared is also a key element in complex learning, and thus the development of buddy lists in instant messaging and the distributed cognition approach found in many social software approaches would be beneficial.

Problem-based learning

Although many of the conventional tools found in VLEs would still be desirable in any PBL approach, for example structuring of resources, group management and assessment, there is often a strong collaborative element to this approach, and thus any of the social tools that facilitate this would be of additional benefit. Instant messaging in particular is a useful 'just-in-time' collaborative tool, so students can ask peers who are online questions at the time they encounter the problem.

Collaborative learning

As with peer learning, this approach is one that could benefit from the newer tools. Whereas peer learning tends to be more informal, collaborative learning will usually be based around a more specific task. In order to promote collaborative learning in this more formal context, structured conferencing tools such as Rotisserie could be used. An activity could be based around students sharing experiences related to an initial statement (for example, 'Describe a memorable learning experience you have had') and then another student allocated to analyse or comment on the first student's response, (for example, 'Analyse the learning experience in light of the theories of learning styles we have covered'), and so on.

In addition, tools such as instant messaging can be used to facilitate the group process. In particular some elements of collaborative process are better realized in real time and others asynchronously. For example, determining roles and breaking down the tasks requires intensive discussion which can become unnecessarily protracted through asynchronous discussion, and thus the use of an instant messaging (or chat room) session to determine these at the start of the project would be beneficial to the group. After this, as individuals work on separate tasks, asynchronous communication is more suitable.

Maintaining a group blog or wiki is also a powerful means of providing a group focus, sharing information and establishing a group identity.

Instructor-led learning

As with content-led, this approach is well catered for by existing VLE tools. However, a number of newer tools could be used in addition to these. For example, regular instant messaging sessions might be a useful means of conducting tutorials. Podcasting represents an excellent means of updating and distributing material to students, which is relatively easy for the educator to achieve on their own. Similarly the maintenance of a blog acts as a method of disseminating newer or additional information.

Technology trends

In this section we have looked at a number of newer technologies including blogs, wikis, podcasting, social software, structured conferencing, instant messaging and e-portfolios. The function of this chapter was not necessarily to describe how these technologies should be used in education, but rather to demonstrate two principles: the manner in which existing technologies can be adopted within an educational context, and how the features of particular technologies can support the requirements of different pedagogies.

The technologies selected here will change, and a completely different set of technologies could have been selected, but they demonstrate some trends which may be significant in education. These can be summarized as:

- **Technologies are not developed for use within education.** Much of educational technology has been developed specifically for use within an educational context, be it for an individual course such as a simulation or an enterprise system such as a VLE. The pervasiveness of the internet and personal computing has raised the general level of technical familiarity and competence, and thus it is increasingly the case that learners come to their education with a wealth of experience in using tools, and preferences for particular technologies. This can be seen as an opportunity within education to leverage robust technologies, which have a strong user base, for educational purposes, rather than the opposite process of creating specific tools and then attempting to convince learners of their worth.

- **There is a move towards socially focused tools and away from content-focused ones.** Many of the technologies here emphasize dialogue, or at least the creation of social content. This can be seen as one reason why the technologies featured in this chapter would be favoured by many of the more revolutionary educators, who also tend to favour social constructivism.
- **Technologies move from niche to mainstream in a short time frame.** Some of the technologies featured here, such as blogging and podcasting, became widespread very quickly. This demonstrates both their ease of use and their fundamental appeal. It also illustrates that there is a base level of technical knowledge amongst the general population, which such technologies build upon. As mentioned above, it is more practical for those within education to take advantage of this, rather than to create new technologies which do not exploit these existing skills.
- **The tools occupy a specific communication niche.** Asynchronous text-based conferencing has often been used as a technology for all communication needs, but many of the technologies here can be seen as meeting specific communication needs. This is again achievable because of an underlying familiarity with standard internet technologies, such as the web and email. Thus blogging, instant messaging, wikis and podcasting all have particular features which suit different types of communication, and thus to fulfil the range of communication needs any individual has they will adopt specific technologies from a suite of tools with which they are familiar.

From a VLE perspective each of these technologies could migrate into an overarching VLE architecture, and be seen as part of the tool set offered within an institutional system. There may be some difficulties with more client-based technologies, such as instant messaging, because the VLE relies on a common web browser interface rather than specific software clients installed on the individual's computer, but some degree of integration is still possible. The issue for VLEs is not to what extent integration is technically feasible, but rather the degree to which it is *desirable*. Rather than imposing technical solutions on learners, or at the higher granularity of the individual educator who is designing an activity, it may become increasingly the case that they select the tools they feel are most appropriate from a range. We shall revisit this approach to technology selection when we look at personal learning environments (PLE) in a later chapter.

Conclusion

In this chapter we have seen how the eight pedagogies set out in Chapter 3 can be supported by a range of non-VLE technologies. In each case specific features of the technologies can be utilized to facilitate the key aspects of the pedagogy for both distance and blended learners. Whereas the common VLE tools tended to favour the more content-focused approaches, many of the newer technologies tend to support more socially oriented approaches. This may just represent the development priorities of VLEs thus far – providing effective means of delivering content was the initial aim, but now they can begin to focus on different types of communication technologies. Most of these technologies can be integrated within existing VLE architectures.

Although the tools in this chapter demonstrate a growing familiarity with internet technologies, there are still strong arguments for an enterprise solution to e-learning technologies. These include the ability to integrate technologies and data in one platform, being able to provide a guaranteed level of provision, centralization of support and development resources and a single system to integrate with other university systems. Assuming then that an institutional solution is required, the next chapter will look at the process of selecting a VLE for an institution.

Chapter 5

Choosing a VLE

At the risk of rendering this whole chapter redundant, the important thing to recognize about choosing a VLE is that it is the making of the decision that is the most significant part of the process, not the actual decision itself. As Graham Greene (1939) put it, 'you've got to choose some line of action and live by it. Otherwise nothing matters at all.' Quite. That is not to say the process of selecting a particular VLE is not important, but it often assumes too much significance in the overall process of integrating e-learning practice within an institution. There is an 'install it and they will come' attitude that underlies much of this as if once the correct purchase is made, all else will follow automatically. However, the reverse is often true, and almost regardless of which technical solution is chosen it is other contextual factors that will determine its success, for instance the suitability and demand from learners, the support from management, staff development programmes, staff enthusiasm, etc. Of course, the qualifier 'almost' is significant in the preceding sentence – if an institution has very particular needs (for example a medical school) or there is a bias towards a particular system (for instance one that has been developed in house) then the choice of system is itself a factor in the overall success.

Even if the actual decision does not have a major influence in the overall success of e-learning implementation, the *process* through which that decision is made is significant. Choosing a VLE usually requires consultation across all units in an institution and thus represents an opportunity to engage a wide variety of users in the wider e-learning dialogue. It can seem as though the broader discussions detract from the more focused task of choosing a VLE, but this may well be the most beneficial aspect of the decision process. It does require immediate continuation of the process, however, and there is sometimes a lull in between the decision making process and the use of the platform while the system is purchased and installed. It is worthwhile maintaining the momentum of the overall e-learning engagement process during this period.

In this chapter I will set out a decision making process that considers the broader context within which the VLE will operate. This is only one realization of such a process, and some alternative methods are mentioned at the end of the chapter. The process has six stages:

1 Devise scenarios appropriate for your organization.
2 Engage in stakeholder consultation.
3 Perform an internal and external review.
4 Devise a set of general principles.
5 Draw up a feature list.
6 Map to strategic objectives.

We will look at each of these in detail now, and an example of the process conducted at the Open University is given in Chapter 12.

Devising scenarios

The role of narrative

In the previous two chapters I set out a number of pedagogies that a VLE might need to support. These can be framed within scenarios which can be viewed as a form of story, or narrative. There are particular advantages to deploying narrative within the process. It has long been a tool in education, particularly that of children, who have a well-developed understanding of, and familiarity with, narrative, since they have usually been exposed to it since birth. This provides a useful framework which teachers can use to their benefit. Teachers use narrative to teach children difficult concepts and to bring structure to the curriculum (Egan 1988).

The use of narrative as an educational tool is often less explicit in tertiary education but it is still prevalent. McCloskey (1990) suggests that there are two dominant ways by which people come to understand a topic – by metaphor or narrative (or models and histories) – and that different fields tend to be dominated by one mode, for instance metaphors dominate physics while narrative dominates biology. Jerome Bruner (1996: 97) has been a long-time advocate of the use of narrative in education, particularly science education. He has proposed three primitive forms of 'meaning-making' which involve an individual's spontaneous inclination to engage in a dialogue with material, to impose some form of organization upon it and to make comparisons with an individual sense of the conventional. He suggests that narrative meets the needs of these three modes well: 'Stories are the vehicles par excellence for entrenching the first three modes of meaning–making into a more structured whole.'

Narrative has a broader significance than education. It has been shown that experts in any field tend to embody their knowledge in the form of narrative (for example, Schon 1983). It can be argued then that to become knowledgeable in a domain is to become familiar with its narratives, and to construct your own relevant ones.

From the perspective of engaging individuals with technology, Fisher (1987) has proposed a 'narrative paradigm' wherein he suggests that stories are the method by which people impose order and reason upon the world. By framing events in a story it permits individuals to interpret their environment, and importantly it provides a framework for making decisions about actions and their likely outcomes.

It thus provides a useful means of framing the rather abstract and dry technical decisions involved in choosing a VLE in terms that non-technical staff can appreciate and engage with.

Developing a range of scenarios

It is first necessary to decide on the pedagogies that need to be explored. These should be described in abstract terms, with underlying philosophy and general principles set out, rather than being specified in terms of a particular course at this stage. I described eight such approaches in Chapter 3, but of course this represents just one particular slice through the range of possible approaches. Each scenario can then be created around one scenario. Again it is preferable for the scenarios not to focus on an existing course, but rather an idealized version that can make multiple demands on technology.

These scenarios can be relatively short, for example for peer learning the following scenario might be proposed as an actual instantiation of the pedagogy:

> Students studying digital photography are introduced to a range of concepts such as lighting, framing, photographing action sequences and using image programmes. For each concept students are asked to submit one or more photographs that illustrate their understanding. Fellow students are required to comment on these as part of the assessment process. The content is developed over the years, using student submissions from previous years to create a database of examples. The assessment is based around student submissions which demonstrate the principles covered. There is also a peer assessment element, where students are required to comment and annotate another student's contribution according to the theory they have studied.

Or they can be longer, based around different perspectives, for example, consider the following one from the perspective of a student:

> Sally is studying psychology with the University of Phoenix. She is on her third course. She is also taking an outside module in Greek language, offered by Stanford University. Her credit for this course will be automatically transferred to Phoenix. Stanford and Phoenix are part of a consortium that allows students to take courses offered by one of the other

institutions, while remaining a student of the main university. Registration, fees, and credit are all handled by the main university, although tuition and support is provided by the partner.

Sally works for an international shipping agency and often has to travel, mainly to Greece. She has a laptop, work machine and mobile device for accessing the internet. She receives an email at work which has been redirected from her Phoenix account. It tells her some new material is available, so she logs in to the Phoenix VLE through a browser.

There is a personalized message telling her that some remedial material on information processing models is available. She took a formative online assessment yesterday, and scored poorly in this subject, so the system has automatically released some new content, which might improve her understanding. She also has a message from her tutor. She is particularly interested in language development in children and has requested more material on this. The tutor has also released some additional content for her to view.

There is also an automatically generated reminder in her calendar that her third assignment is due next week. The course chair has put a flag in to say there is an interesting programme on the Discovery channel tonight. She has also put in a reminder for herself to contact the members of her group for their collaborative task.

She sets aside an hour for herself at work and looks at the additional material she has received. There are four resources for the information processing subject area:

- a simulation demonstrating different processing models from Indiana University;
- an alternative textual description from a text book;
- an interview with an expert by one of the course team;
- a wiki document based on student discussion around an article.

Estimated study times are given with the resources and she likes to be active in her learning, so she chooses the simulation. This opens up in a new window, and after quickly skimming the tutorial she explores two different models. She thinks she has a better understanding now, so decides to test this by taking the formative test again. This generates some new questions in this area, which include multiple choice, short text answers and image interpretation. She achieves a decent score on this and so decides to leave this session.

As she is logging out her instant messaging client tells her that Steve has logged on. Steve has been on many of the same courses and they have become friends. She says hello to him and they have a synchronous chat. They talk about the baseball last night and then about the course. They exchange some ideas about the forthcoming assignment, and then Sally has to go.

Later that evening Sally logs in from home. She sees her reminder about contacting her group, which has been arranged for 7.30 that evening. She plugs in her web cam and goes to the designated address for the collaborative session. Ramon is already logged in, and has uploaded the task document. Soon Ramlesh and Katryn join in. John can't make it, but has sent an email with his thoughts. They discuss the task, which is to produce a research proposal in a subject from the course. This group has come together because they all have an interest in child language development. They have all put in proposals, and decide that Ramlesh's one looking at causal connectives will be best. They have to allocate roles, as specified in the task. Katryn will do the literature review, Ramlesh the methodology, Ramon will offer a critique of the proposal, while Sally will act as the reporter and project manager. John has offered to write the final proposal and be responsible for its submission as a joint work. They agree a schedule, which Sally enters into their calendars. They say goodbye and log off.

Sally watches the TV programme recommended by the course chair. While doing so she has her mobile device with her and makes some notes in her online blog, which she uses as a study journal.

A week later Sally is in Greece. She uses her mobile device to interact with her group and read the course material. She avoids any heavy multimedia which does not display well on this device. She drags these into her calendar, however, to remind her to look at them when she gets back home.

Her assignment is due. This is to create a multimedia resource for other students on a subject covered in the course. They have been provided with a range of resources (video clips, images, articles, etc.), plus access to a variety of online repositories and an online tool for creating the finished resource using drag and drop. Sally has been working on a resource about the evolutionary basis for language development. She has included video clips of vervet monkeys communicating different calls and a two-year-old child talking. She includes some images and graphs, as well as links to six articles. She completes her 1,500 words explaining these and submits the assignment. The resource will form part of a repository that future students can use, just as she has been looking at resources from previous cohorts. These are all automatically tagged so they can be searched and they can also be browsed by subjects. Students can add comments and ratings to them also.

Further scenarios from the perspective of educators, administrative staff, different types of students, etc can also be created.

The use of scenarios has two main functions:

1 As a device for determining technical functionality.
2 As a means of engaging users in the stakeholder's consultation.

In order to realize the first of these functions, it is necessary to work through each scenario specifying what would be the role of VLE in the scenario. For example, the peer learning scenario given above might lead to the following description of the VLE role:

> As well as supporting content in a range of media, the VLE would need to provide a peer assessment tool that supported the random allocation of a marker to each assignment and provided tools for annotating images. An archived repository is also required, which is searchable by metadata, and thus tools which allow students to easily submit their images to such a repository would be necessary. General collaborative tools such as instant messaging, video conferencing and shared areas would also facilitate peer to peer discussion. Such a scenario may be an example where specific tools that require a client, such as image editing software, need to exist outside of the VLE, because they offer functionality which is fundamental to the course and are inefficient to deliver online, and thus the loss of integration is acceptable.

Disadvantages

Although the use of scenarios has a number of benefits, the approach also has some disadvantages which it is worth highlighting, as complementary methods may then be used to lessen the effect of these.

The first of these is that they are necessarily limited in their scope. This is a direct result of their utility as a sense-making procedure – in order to make sense of a complex world we impose a narrative on it, which helps to simplify that complexity. This is a useful means of imposing order and causality on an otherwise unstructured and unconnected set of events, but it also means that some detail is omitted in order to fit in to the narrative, and other factors are only considered in the limited sense in which they can be accommodated within the narrative. So, any scenario we construct about the use of technology in education will always be leaving out more than it contains, as it could not possibly include every possible use, context and user within it. In order to reduce this simplification effect it is necessary to create a range of scenarios that at least address different areas of the problem space, but one simply needs to acknowledge that this is a restricted view.

Related to this is the tendency for scenarios to reflect the views and bias of those who create them. Thus they are often utopian or dystopian in nature, which will then either concentrate excessively on the negative aspects of the technology (and thus promote the status quo which is the ultimate goal of the dystopians) or ignore real issues in the potential use of the technology (and thus promote a very radical technical solution which is the underlying goal of the utopians). These effects can also be reduced by getting a range of users to generate scenarios, using a template and guidelines for their creation.

Stakeholder consultation

The term stakeholders carries some political connotations or is seen as indicative of the type of 'management speak' that pervades much of education, and thus raises suspicion in some. Sternberg suggests that the definition of the term has changed over recent years:

> Originally, stakeholders were identified as those without whom an organization could not survive, those in whom the organization had a stake. Now, in contrast, stakeholders are more commonly identified as those who have a stake in an organization. This represents a radical shift, from those who affect the organization, to those who are affected by it.
>
> (Sternberg 1997: 3)

She goes on to highlight one of the main defects in the stakeholder approach in that it stresses equality amongst stakeholders, which may paralyze decision making or lead to a bland, or the least contentious, option which may not be the best decision in the longer term. She argues that

> the definitive stakeholder aim – balancing benefits for all stakeholders – precludes all objectives which favour particular groups. . . . Stakeholder theory does not indicate which of these benefits is to be preferred, or how conflicting interests are to be balanced. Are stakeholder interests all strictly equal? Are some more important than others? If so, which are they?
>
> (Sternberg 1997: 4)

There may be some validity in these complaints, particularly with regards to businesses, but when dealing with a complex system such as a VLE, which has users from multiple perspectives and thus has to satisfy a variety of objectives, some consultation with these different user groups is essential. In contrast to Sternberg, Beierle (2002) found that in the majority of cases where it had occurred, stakeholder consultation (in environmental planning) improved the quality of decisions by adding new information, ideas and analysis, and indeed there was a correlation between the intensity of the stakeholder consultation and the resulting quality of the decision.

One of the concerns about stakeholder consultation is that many of those who constitute stakeholders lack some of the scientific or technical knowledge to fully understand the issues. However, this should be seen as a virtue – the open source community has long recognized the value in different types of expertise and inputs in developing software. Inexperienced users, for example, are often the best people to find bugs in software because they use it in unpredictable ways; as Weber (2004: 78) puts it, 'different people doing different things with the software will surface more bugs'. The danger in not going through a stakeholder consultation is that you seek feedback from like-minded people.

As well as improving the potential quality of the decision, the other main benefit in conducting a stakeholder consultation exercise is that it begins to engage a range of users with the broader context within which the VLE will operate. At the start of this chapter I suggested that the *process* of VLE selection was as important as, if not more important than, the actual decision itself. This is particularly true with the stakeholder consultation. Much of what comes out of such an exercise will not relate directly to a VLE – for example, many users will not have sufficient knowledge to provide a list of required features. However, they will be able to express areas of concern and enthusiasm about the potential deployment of a VLE, and thus the process is essential in establishing a more holistic conceptualization of the environment within which the VLE will function. This should feed into the implementation plan, and thus help remove some of the potential obstacles to its successful deployment.

By using techniques such as the scenario-based approach, it is possible to gain feedback on specific features as well as the broader issues. It is in the stakeholder consultation that the potential of a narrative-based approach to facilitate engagement with technology and create a shared notion of a desirable future which can be articulated by all stakeholders is realized.

The range of stakeholders that need to be consulted will vary according to the circumstances of any institution, but they will probably include the following:

- Students – it may be necessary to ensure that an appropriate cross-section of students are consulted, for example there may be different needs based on study mode (campus-based, distance, part-time), age/experience, subject area, disability, etc.
- Academic staff – again different groups may provide different feedback, and the specific needs of subject areas will be most keenly felt by this group, as well as potential differences between teaching and research-focused staff, part-time and full-time members, external consultants, etc. The function of the VLE may determine the type of output from this section of stakeholders (or in turn the function may be determined by consultation with this group). For example, if the VLE is also intended to act as the technology through which research interests are shared, i.e. to act as a virtual research environment (VRE) also, then this will produce another set of needs from the stakeholder consultation. Similarly if the VLE is meant to act as the main staff information channel, that is an institutional intranet or as the main student information source for administrative needs, then the demands on that system will be different to those on a pure learning environment.

- Technical staff – this group will have the task of implementing a VLE in a technical sense, and integrating it with existing institutional systems. They will also have considerable experience with previous systems. There may also be very specific technical constraints which will influence the final decision, for example underlying hardware or database systems.
- Administrative staff – a VLE will need to interface with a number of administrative systems, and so the boundaries between these will be important in the everyday operations undertaken by administrative staff, for example they need to be assured that data is consistent between the two systems, so when a change is made in one it is reflected in the other. The VLE will also be a system which has varying levels of significance for students and so those administrators with a student-facing role will need to be familiar with the system as it may generate queries. The VLE may also be the route through which administrative information is conveyed to students.
- Support staff – technical support, those with a staff development remit and pastoral student support staff will have specific needs and interests in relation to a VLE. These will include political and financial issues such as the intended extent to which it will be used (an optional, peripheral system generates fewer issues than a central, compulsory one), available resources (for instance in relation to a helpdesk, or staff development programme) and implementation timetable. They will also cover areas such as the ease of use of any system, available training materials and possible support from the vendor or consultants.
- Senior management – the executive of the institution are likely to have very specific expectations of a VLE. Depending on how they view e-learning in general they may see it anywhere from a necessary evil, which might be summarized as 'everyone else has got one so we have to have one', to a crucial component in meeting the strategic directives of the institution, whereby they foresee e-learning as a vital element in meeting the needs of students and reaching new audiences. They will also have their own agenda(s), sometimes conflicting between themselves, regarding finances, staffing, timing, implementation strategy, and so on. One of the common complaints about VLEs is that they are in essence a management tool that facilitates greater centralization and control of the teaching process. Thus the degree to which all stakeholders' views are considered in the final VLE decision and is not skewed to the needs of senior management will be crucial in its ultimate success.

The timing of the stakeholder consultation is a difficult issue, and is perhaps best viewed as an iterative process. Some of the decisions regarding the VLE may be a result of the consultation, and it will also be necessary to frame elements of the consultation within a set framework to move dialogue forward and not simply reiterate arguments about the relative merits of e-learning in general.

Perform an internal and external review

Much of the review process may well be taking place in parallel with the stakeholder consultation, as it may aid the process of defining the framework mentioned above. For example, if an external review concludes that there is little demand for e-learning in the main subject areas or amongst the demographics the institution specializes in, then this may well place some constraints upon the budget and resources allocated to the VLE project. Similarly, if a technical internal review reveals that any system not based on Oracle databases, say, will necessitate the purchase of new underlying systems and there is a lack of expertise in other databases, then this may act as a preliminary filter to any VLE purchase.

From these two examples it is obvious that what can be covered in a review can be varied. A review differs from the broader stakeholder consultation in that it is more focused, and often conducted by specialists, who may be internal to the institution or external consultants. The type of external reviews that may be useful are:

- Market – an analysis of the potential market for e-learning or blended courses.
- Technical developments – what is the current technical context, are there specific trends developing, or technologies emerging that will have a significant impact upon the VLE project?
- Products – a review and comparison of the common VLE solutions, including open source and commercial options.
- Case studies – experience from other institutions in their choice and implementation of a system.

The sort of reviews that might be carried out internal to the institution include:

- Current e-learning practice – what are people currently doing and what are the main issues they have encountered?
- Technical audit – what software and systems are currently in use? This would encompass some of the current practice mentioned above, but also other systems that the VLE would need to interact with, such as student databases. Any projected purchases or development of relevant systems should also be uncovered at this stage, and contact points with other teams and projects established.
- Financial review – the financial climate within which the VLE will operate will have a significant impact. For instance if there is a projected shortfall in student numbers, then the likely resources allocated to the implementation of an enterprise-wide system may be limited. In this case a more modest, limited roll-out would be advisable, targeting certain subject areas where there is likely to be most benefit.

As with the stakeholder analysis the problem with the review process is the relative significance of each input. There may be conflicting recommendations from each of these review inputs, for example the external technical review may be suggesting that the general trends are at odds with the internal technical expertise. Unfortunately there is no reliable means of resolving these conflicts, as the weight that should be attached to each recommendation will vary across institutions and over time. Even within each review the importance of any one recommendation will vary, for example the financial review may make some relatively minor suggestions, but have an absolute budget limit, which will influence the decision. At this stage careful negotiation and discussion with senior management is required to weight the various factors appropriately. The strategic direction of the institution is likely to be significant in performing this task, and we will look at these in the last stage of our VLE process.

In the next two chapters we will look at some of the factors that may arise from the review process by examining the other systems that need to integrate with a VLE and the development of educational technology standards.

Devise a set of aims and general principles

Having performed at least one round of stakeholder consultation, conducted a number of reviews and created a set of e-learning scenarios, the next stage is to devise a set of general principles. It is possible to go straight to the next stage, and draw up a list of specific features, but it is worth devising principles at one level of abstraction first, as these will inform the implementation strategy and the future direction of the VLE project. Any institution embarking on the implementation of a VLE needs to view it as an ongoing process, as technology and teaching practice develop. Devising a set of general principles that constitute the vision of the VLE project therefore fulfils several functions:

- it provides a set of guidelines for future decisions, since within the overall VLE project there may be a number of sub-projects;
- it lends some transparency to the decision making process;
- it communicates the underlying philosophy and approach of the project;
- it synthesizes and concludes the first part of the process and thus demonstrates that the various inputs have been considered.

The aims should focus on what the VLE will seek to provide for the institution, for instance they might be phrased in rather general terms such as ‘to increase the value of the online learning experience to the learner’ or with more specific goals, such as ‘to deliver 50 per cent of courses online in the next five years’.

The principles will be at a more operational level and will thus aid the development process. They might include specific technological approaches, for example 'Implementation should follow a service-oriented approach', reference to external developments, for example 'Adoption of educational technology standards where appropriate' or formalization of a commitment to certain principles, for example 'Be tested for accessibility and at a minimum conform to Web Accessibility Initiative (WAI) priority 1 and 2 guidelines (http://www.w3.org/WAI/)'.

Draw up a feature list

Armed with the outputs from the previous four phases, it is now possible to draw up a list of desired features that the VLE would need to possess. By examining the outputs from each of these phases and converting them into specific features, a comprehensive list can be drawn up, with each feature described according to a template. The template adopted during the process at the Open University was as follows:

Description: A brief description of the tool or requirement.

Current provision: How the requirement is currently met within the institution, if at all.

Related projects: Any current projects underway that have relevance to this requirement.

Issues: Some comments on issues relating to the requirement.

Priority: This was given on a scale of 1 to 3, with 1 meaning that it should be addressed in the short term, 2 as medium term and 3 being desirable but not urgent.

Ease of implementation: This addressed how easy any service would be to implement. This could be a result of having the tool or data already available, or being relatively easy to implement. Again a scale of 1 (easy or quick to implement) to 3 (implementation would require significant development work) was used.

Scope: The VLE cuts across many different domains and so while many functions are seen as being part of the VLE, they are not directly in scope for the project team. This specified whether the task was fully within the remit of the VLE team, partially in collaboration with another team, or outside of the VLE's scope, but something that they needed to be aware of.

An example then might be as follows:

Personal log and notes tool

Description: Each user has access to a personal log and notes tool which allows free entry of textual and graphical information. Users can use this tool to make notes.

Personal log and note entries can be attached to learning content delivered by the VLE. There would need to be a realistic size limit placed on the notes available to each student.

Current provision: Some bespoke development for specific courses.
Related projects: Blogging tool, development of e-portfolio.
Issues: This will need to be allocated to individuals, and not by course, since they will take notes with them. The notes should be easily extractable so they can be transferred to another system. The extent to which the related projects meet the needs of this tool needs to be determined, as a proliferation of tools performing similar functions will lead to confusion.
Priority: 2
Ease of implementation: 1 (for simple tool), 2 for a more e-portfolio-based solution.
Scope: In scope.

This feature list then embodies the pedagogic, technical and strategic requirements, and can be used as a means of scoring possible VLE products.

Map to strategic directives

Throughout the process the strategic direction of the institution will have been exerting an influence, either directly or indirectly. It is therefore something that needs to be acknowledged early on, as it will influence a number of decisions, such as the priority of the features described above. However, it is worth setting it out as an explicit stage, as this will both help inform the final decision, and also clarify the position of the VLE in relation to the institution's overall mission. It may be necessary to determine the strategic directives of the institution, in which case this should form part of the stakeholder process, with particular involvement required from senior management.

The exercise of mapping a potential VLE onto the strategic objectives can then be performed, by stating how, if at all, a VLE could support or influence them. A realistic assessment is necessary during this process if the VLE is not to be set unachievable targets and thus ultimately doomed to failure. For example, a strategic directive might be to increase student retention, and a VLE could make a claim to improving retention rates through the use of technologies such as student tracking to identify problems early on, self assessment to reinforce understanding and increase motivation, allowing selective release of content suited to needs and experience, and so on. However, it would be rash to claim that the presence of a VLE alone will increase retention rates by a set amount, as the reasons students cease study are varied and complex, and thus the VLE would only be one part of an overall strategy to address student drop-out. It may also be that other directives conflict with this, for example, the desire to expand student numbers or reach new audiences may result in a student cohort with different needs, where retention rates are much lower.

Thus the aim of this stage is to situate the VLE in relation to the overall direction and imperatives of an institution. Part of this function is to raise awareness of how a VLE can have an impact across an institution, which may aid its acceptance in the implementation phase, but care should be taken not to position it as a technological panacea.

Other approaches

The approach set out in this chapter is only one take on the VLE selection process. Its strength is in its recognition of the selection process as part of a much wider e-learning strategy. It has weaknesses also; for instance it is a less technically focused approach than some others, and it does not address an implementation strategy.

There are a number of other suggested approaches and case studies, all of which have their own advantages and disadvantages. As with the ultimate choice of a VLE, perhaps the most important contribution of these approaches is to simply select one of them and have a methodology that can be followed and discussed.

Other approaches tend to focus more around the comparison of existing products, for example Chohan (2001) suggests the following approach for the selection of an MLE, based on their experience at Leeds college:

1 Identify the need for an MLE. What will you use it for, who will be the students, how will you use it?
2 Devise criteria with which to compare MLEs.
3 Create a shortlist.
4 Investigate the shortlisted companies.
5 Make final recommendations.

Alvardo (2004) has a similar approach, recommending seven steps to selecting an LMS:

1 Determine the learning strategy.
2 Document requirements.
3 Research LMS companies.
4 Prepare the request for proposal (RFP).
5 Review the proposals.
6 Schedule meetings and demos.
7 Make the selection.

And there are many more approaches, with varying degrees of thoroughness and with different perspectives. The JISC MLE toolkit (Liber and Holyfield

2006) is a useful resource for a very comprehensive approach, and Edutools (2006) have a good comparison list for available systems.

The approaches are not solution neutral, however, and to some degree the selection process will favour certain outcomes. For instance, the procedures recommended by both Alavardo and Chohan are oriented towards the *procurement* of a VLE. The approach is thus unlikely to recommend a service oriented solution that requires some in-house integration, and will probably favour commercial VLEs over open source ones, as commercial companies are more practised at working with the procurement process (there are some commercial providers of open source VLEs however). This probably reflects an underlying assumption about the type of solution that is desired, but those assumptions are not made explicit in the process itself.

Conclusion

In this chapter a six-stage process for determining a VLE solution has been described. As well as reaching a decision regarding a technology, the process represents an opportunity to engage a wide variety of stakeholders in discussion about e-learning in general, and thus the context within which the VLE will be operating. The use of narrative or scenarios as a means of engaging stakeholders and users with issues surrounding the technology was stressed, and also the need to map any longer term VLE decisions to the institution's strategic direction, or mission.

When looking at other approaches it is clear that the process that is chosen may itself have an influence on the eventual outcome, by favouring certain conclusions. By at least making a specific mapping onto strategic directives, the process outlined in this chapter does allow for some recognition of a bias towards a certain flavour of solution. This bias, or strategic leaning, will often be captured in the institution's attitude towards open source software, which some see as an important strategic, financial or even moral direction, and others view as merely one possible option amongst many. We will look in more detail at this debate in a later chapter. In the next chapter we will consider the other systems with which a VLE will need to interact, as these will play a significant part in the overall success of the VLE, but they also help to elicit some further appreciation of how e-learning is envisaged within an institution.

Chapter 6

MLEs and metaphors

In Chapter 1 the concept of managed learning environments (MLEs) was introduced. The motivation behind this term was the recognition that, in order to be effective, a VLE needed to integrate with a number of other institutional systems, most of which would be legacy systems. In this chapter we will look at the relationship with some of these systems, and also at issues surrounding the language we use to talk about complex systems such as MLEs which are essentially hybrid in nature, consisting of a number of largely autonomous sub-systems.

The typical systems that any VLE needs to 'talk' to include:

- Portal – web-based system for non-course related information.
- Content management system – a system that stores, organizes, tracks and manages various types of content that can be used in a VLE.
- Student records system – contains details of student details, including personal details, assessment record, finance history, study history, etc.
- Library systems – including journal databases, catalogues, lending history, course related resources, etc.

In addition there will be a number of course specific tools which may not be part of a standard VLE across an institution, but which any one course may wish to utilize. The issue is to what extent the VLE is aware of them, or they are considered stand alone.

One of the problems with realizing an MLE is what might be termed 'feature annexation'. As developers seek to make their products more attractive there is a tendency to increase the range of functionality they offer. Each system therefore seeks to annex some of the tools, features or functions offered by other systems. Thus, instead of having a clean architecture with neatly defined boundaries, as we see in Figure 6.1, we have a more complex picture, which might be akin to that depicted in Figure 6.2, where there is overlap of functionality. In this version it is possible for any component to expand or reduce in size, depending on the functions it is assigned.

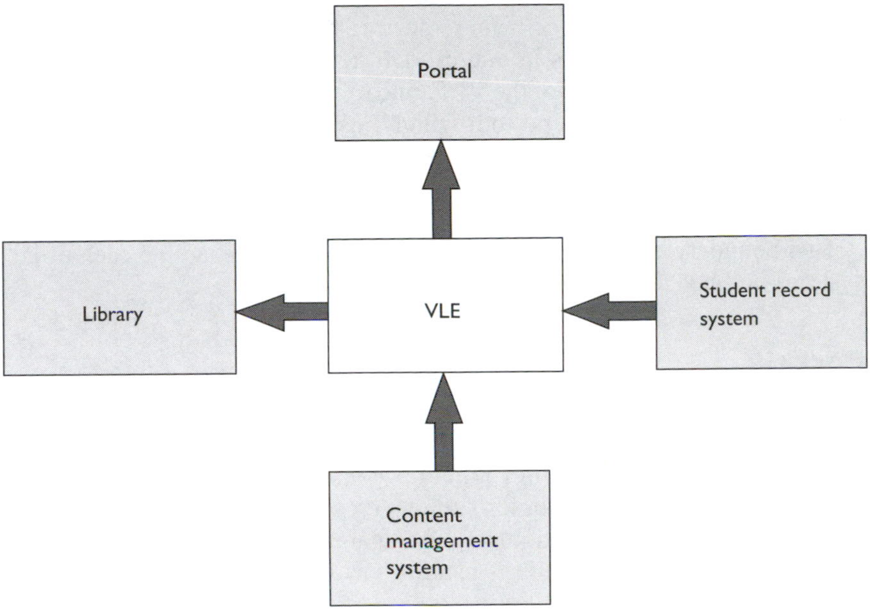

Figure 6.1 An MLE can be conceptualized as having distinct boundaries between components.

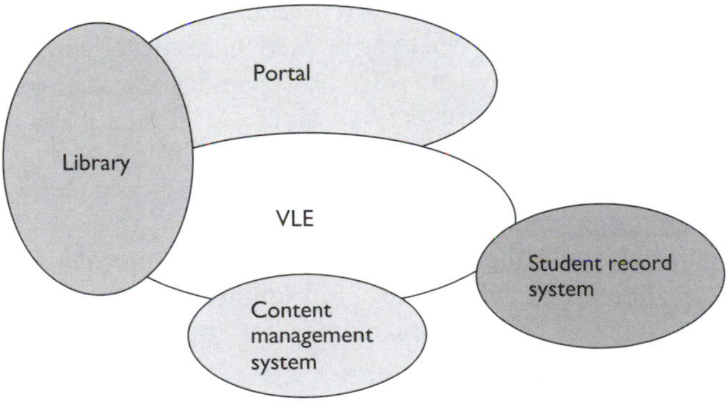

Figure 6.2 There is considerable overlap in functionality within an MLE, where the boundaries and relative significance of any subsystem is subject to change.

A small example might be seen with the development of e-portfolio tools, which we looked at in Chapter 4. As these develop there is an increasing functionality bleed from VLEs, with e-portfolios containing tools for asynchronous communication, note-taking, blogs, resource gathering and assessment tools. On the assumption that having different tools for the same function will be confusing to users and lead to a variation in practice that would be difficult to support (an assumption that some would challenge, I should point out), then implementers need to decide in which system these functions will reside. Thus in one model the e-portfolio system grows in significance, at the expense of the VLE, and in another version the e-portfolio system is seen as a peripheral tool which links in to the VLE. These technological power struggles will be reflected in political ones within the institution, particularly if different teams are responsible for the various tools and a clear architecture and approach have not been agreed on previously.

This boundary confusion will become evident as we examine each of the systems outlined above in more detail.

Portals

The JISC (2003) define a portal as a

> network service that brings together content from diverse distributed resources using technologies such as cross searching, harvesting, and alerting, and collates this into an amalgamated form for presentation to the user. This presentation is usually via a web browser, though other means are also possible. For users, a portal is a, possibly personalised, common point of access where searching can be carried out across one or more than one resource and the amalgamated results viewed.

In the commercial sector, portals are often seen as an extension to the company's intranet. By linking a portal to an underlying content management system content can be served up dynamically, and updated by a range of users who have responsibility for their respective areas. A portal can be just a collection of links, and sometimes the term is used to refer to a website that collects together information from different sources and acts as a gateway to other sites, but with no personalization.

In educational use, however, the term has become more specifically focused on a personalized site, which acts as the main online point of contact for students. One can identify five key principles for the use of portals in education:

1 Personalization is the key concept. Although the term portal is often used indiscriminately, in education terms the key benefit it offers is personalization for students. It may seem trivial, but the addition of the determiner 'My' captures much of this, and many universities use this to brand their portal, for example MyYale, MyUCLA, etc. By providing a set of channels that can be configured according to a student's data, and customized according to their preferences, a high degree of personalization and relevance can be attained. This can be seen as a direct descendant of the MySpace phenomenon found in general internet usage.

2 Portals are often seen as a key component in an institution's e-strategy. Portals are not merely another technology project, but often seen as a key change factor and technology in the implementation of an overall e-strategy.
3 There is a shift of focus to self-sufficiency, reduction in paper and manual entry. A number of portal projects claim that one of the benefits of implementing a portal was the reduction in administrative costs, largely because these processes are automated and responsibility passes to the student. Such functions include payments, maintaining personal details, course choice, etc.
4 They usually link to an external VLE. The VLE is the more established technology and most institutions have maintained a fairly clear division between the two systems.
5 They have a unified architecture and approach. Where portals have been adopted the same technology is used for staff and all students. Once information channels have been determined, providing a different view on these is not problematic and is the most efficient means of operation.

There is a good deal of information that is relevant to students, but is ill-suited to the more course-oriented VLE system, as it needs to be either persistent across all courses, or targeted to specific individuals. For example, student handbooks and regulations, faculty or school information, news regarding clubs and interest groups, would all fit awkwardly within a system designed to manage users according to courses. There can often be an element of forcing a system to perform a task for which it is not designed, for example by creating a 'course' for all students in one school, so that level of information can be disseminated. It is more suitable to adopt a portal approach for such information as these systems are designed to allow customizable and personalized information feeds.

If one thinks of a portal as a set of information containers, then those containers can be configured to receive information that is determined either by the institution or the user, and usually a mixture of these two. Thus a portal might contain:

- institutional news which all students receive;
- subject area information which is determined by their chosen course(s);
- an email account through which they receive announcements;
- news feeds from third-party sources (such as the BBC), which are set at defaults but can be chosen by the user;
- feeds from social areas such as clubs;
- a range of static information such as university regulations and personal details, which can be amended;
- discussion areas for social or non-course related subjects;
- links to other university systems such as the library, and a course specific area.

By populating the channels with different information feeds, the same technology can be used for staff, visitors, part-time tutors, etc. What it requires, however, is that all the units responsible for disseminating information do so in a format that a portal can use, for example RSS. For staff who have been accustomed to using other means, for example they have developed their own website, then there will be issues of ownership and protection of existing systems. Working with information feeds that are assembled elsewhere, instead of creating your own information site, requires something of a shift in both the type of content created, which will be much more event driven, and also in style, since the context it is viewed in will be different, so it needs to stand alone. More static information, such as student regulations, is better served by being available as linked resources rather than dynamic feeds. For time-limited, event driven information such as news of lectures or exams, then news feeds are more suitable. There will be information which falls between these two extremes, however, and here the decision is whether the information gains from the presence of being a feed, where a student is unlikely to miss it, or whether it needs to persist beyond the average lifespan of news information, in which case it may be moved down the list as other items come in and thus be lost.

For an institution the portal represents not only a means of conveying appropriate information to different groups of users, but also a means of establishing a relationship with the institution as a whole, and not just with a particular cohort or school. This is given added emphasis for distance or part-time students, who may not have the same affinity with the institution as campus-based students. This is sometimes just interpreted as an exercise in branding, but it has implications for student satisfaction and can impact upon their learning. For students the portal is a representation of the wider support network and the reassurance of belonging to a larger institution. I ran a course that was initially delivered through the UK eUniversities initiative (which itself was really a portal to offerings of other universities), and when this ceased operating students were transferred back into the Open University systems. During a course evaluation we asked students about their experience with the OU's portal, and many reported that, even if they didn't use it, they found its presence reassuring, in comparison with the delivery through the UKeU where they did not have that sense of belonging to a larger institution. One student commented about the portal, 'although I didn't use it much, it was nice to know it was there, I felt part of a university. It was comforting' (Weller *et al.* 2005: 257).

A portal for tools

In terms of the boundary with a VLE, at first glance the division may seem quite clear cut, with institutional level and non-course related information coming through the portal and users going from here to the VLE for their learning and teaching functions. This is how most VLEs and portals are arranged. However, this is to ignore a recent trend in educational technology which we saw in Chapter 3, which suggests that content is usually where the initial effort is focused, but afterwards there is a shift in focus towards tools, dialogue and pedagogy. We saw this with the type of tools currently gaining in popularity, but it can also be seen in the area of educational technology standards. Initial effort was focused on developing standards that would facilitate the exchange of content, for example metadata and content packaging. More recently though efforts have been focused on developing standards that will allow tools to interact, and to specify pedagogy (we will look at these in the next chapter). Portal development is following a similar trend, so portals are seen not just as a means of accessing information from different sources, but also of accessing tools and services from different providers. If one begins to view portals in this respect then there is a good deal of feature annexing from the VLE, and indeed there is a strong argument that the portal level is the more suitable home for some tools. A blog, for example, is the type of tool that has a persistent function that extends beyond any one course. Any course, or module, may ask students to make particular use of it in that context, for example as a study journal, but one of their benefits is that they are focused on the individual and thus represent an ideal tool for maintaining a journal across all courses, and even beyond formal study as a tool for lifelong learners. They are thus much better positioned as part of the provision that is centred on the individual learner and not on one specific course.

This represents a more fundamental revision of how we envisage the provision of technologies to students, which have traditionally focused around courses, even prior to the advent of e-learning; consider how conventional universities formalize the course emphasis in their physical instantiation of lecture halls, laboratories, computer suites, tutor rooms, etc. With e-learning, however, some of the physical and financial constraints that made this a practical means to structure education no longer apply. As Evans and Wurster (2000: 18) put it, 'what is truly revolutionary about the explosion in connectivity is the possibility it offers to unbundle information from its physical carrier'. We can now cluster the technology around the learner, and not around the course, with those technologies persisting across the learner's interaction with the institution and possibly beyond. The function those tools are put to then is not determined solely by educators, but by the learner also, for example an instant messaging client can be used as part of a formal education task and also informally for social communication.

In this possible future the VLE is squeezed between the portal and component tools, to the point that it may no longer be necessary. There are problems with this approach, for instance a portal level integration is often rather 'dumb' about its constituent components – it is merely a container for these. If you wish to have more meaningful integration that would allow a system to manage learning activities, or to track student activity, then a portal approach is probably not suitable. The degree of reengineering required would transform the portal into a VLE, so it would be better to start with the VLE in this instance and add in portal functionality. It seems that one of the consequences of feature annexation is that we may end up reinventing each technology but from a different starting point.

Content management systems

A content management system (CMS), or for educational purposes they are often labelled learning content management system (LCMS), is used for the creation, management, control, retrieval and packaging of a variety of resources.

There are several assumptions underlying an LCMS, which means the decision to purchase one, regardless of which system is deployed, carries political and strategic connotations. For an LCMS to be worthwhile then the following contextual assumptions could be made:

1 Most content is available digitally – this is not too controversial, as all institutions have a good deal of information available digitally, but this is often administrative in nature and may not be the case for the majority of educational material. It may follow then that there is a requirement for all information to be produced in this way.

2 Content is in appropriately sized chunks – without absolutely necessitating a learning object approach, for an LCMS to be useful it needs to store chunks of learning content that can be aggregated together in different packages (usually courses). The granularity of the resources therefore needs to be suitably small to permit this, which has implications for how academics produce material.

3 Reuse of material is encouraged – while an LCMS can be used to create content, and is particularly useful when doing so collaboratively, there is an assumption that the resources within an LCMS will be reused in different contexts. If reuse is not part of the culture then the value to the institution of the LCMS will be diminished.

4 E-learning plays a significant role in the overall educational strategy – this may seem a touch obvious but, as with VLEs, there is a tendency to feel as though everyone else has an LCMS, therefore we need one, regardless of the role it will play in the overall teaching strategy. An LCMS is an expensive and sophisticated system, which requires a critical mass of resources for it to be worth the investment. This assumes that the LCMS is used to support teaching, and is not an institutional CMS for storing and managing mainly internal, administrative documents.

The combined effect of these assumptions represents a significant change in terms of the everyday practice of educators. While an LCMS may seem like just a logical constituent element of the overall MLE, it comes laden with a number of implications. Making these explicit, so they can be addressed, reduced, or increased is probably the best strategy if an LCMS is to provide any return on its investment.

The conventional view of how an LCMS interfaces with a VLE posits the LCMS as the repository store for material, where different versions are created, manipulated and tagged. These are then published out to the VLE, usually in a standard format, for example as an IMS Content Package, which the VLE can then present to learners with all the associated tools.

It will come as no surprise though that this division of responsibility is not the only way to view the relationship between the two systems. At one extreme the LCMS is redundant, and the VLE is effectively used as a content management system. This works well enough if assumptions three and four above are not met, since the VLE can act as a content management system on a local level for individuals or within a school. This approach has the advantage that the VLE is the system educators interact with, so they can upload their content, create folders and share and search for other resources if the system is configured thus without interacting with (yet) another system. However, at an enterprise level across an institution, or more significantly across several institutions, then the VLE is not sophisticated enough in the way it handles the resources. It is also not aimed at supporting the collaborative creative process in the way many LCMSs are. This view of the VLE as LCMS does raise the question to what extent a separate system is required. If feature annexation continues then the VLE will simply absorb the functions of an LCMS, and indeed many current VLEs are sold with an LCMS option.

At the other end of the functional divide, there is the possibility that the LCMS itself acts as a VLE. This might be particularly true for certain types of learning, for example resource based approaches where students are given access to a wide range of resources, or just-in-time learning where appropriate learning objects are delivered to the individual based on their needs. This approach allows for more dynamic delivery of content, as it does not have the publication break between the two systems, so content can be served up as it is required. For personalized learning, then, a more LCMS-centric system will be required. Just as it is possible to ask to what extent a VLE can act as an LCMS, it is worth considering how much effort is required to make an LCMS act as a VLE. In partnership with a portal the VLE can be squeezed, to the point of extinction, between the LCMS and the portal as shown in Figure 6.3. For example, at Cranfield University, Harrison (2004) reports how they used the HarvestRoad CMS to act as their VLE, and that this overcomes some of the problems of conventional VLEs, most notably that of 'islands of content'.

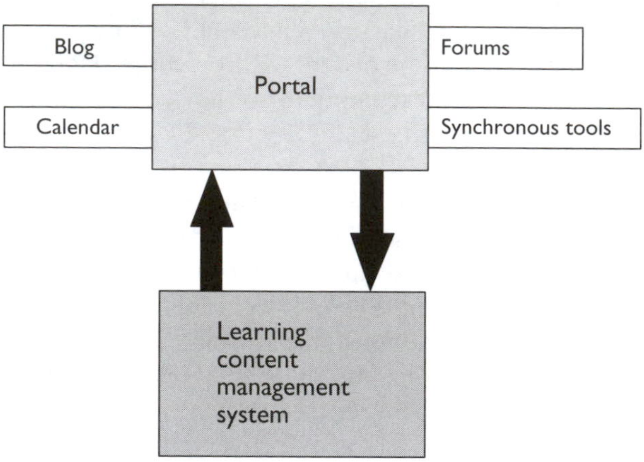

Figure 6.3 In one configuration the portal acts as a portal to tools, and content is served directly from the LCMS.

Student records

Feature annexing is less of an issue with student record systems, although they do represent the main point of integration for any VLE. Integration with other systems is desirable, but it is essential for the student database. A staff database may be part of the same system, or separate, but the issues will be the same. A VLE needs to get the following information from a student record system:

- Personal details.
- Programme of study – as well as the current courses or modules the student is studying, information on the overall programme or study area may be required by a VLE, so that access to appropriate resources and discussion areas is granted.
- Course allocation – which courses the student has access to, which may be in different faculties.
- Roles and permissions – this will map onto roles that are predetermined in the VLE, and allocate certain privileges. For instance, a lecturer will be able to access administrative functions and areas that are out of bounds for a student. The same user may have multiple identities within the VLE, for instance an individual may be a part-time tutor on one course and a student on another.
- Special requirements – details of any special needs or disabilities that have relevance to the VLE may be passed across, although this will be a policy decision. For instance, if a VLE contains alternative content for students with visual impairment, then it can deliver this content as the

default option if it is aware of this for the individual. This is a delicate issue, however, and when information is passed between systems it becomes more difficult to keep track of who can access it.
- Assessment record – the VLE may keep its own log for any student, and thus require history of past study, assessment details, etc.

Most VLEs then store this information internally within their own database. The issue then is one of consistency between the two data stores. This is usually achieved through batch, rather than dynamic, updating, with the emphasis on changes in one environment being replicated in another, while also ensuring that certain data remains secure and reliable, for instance a student can change their preferred name in the VLE, but not their assessment record.

The advent of a web services-type approach may make this duplication of data unnecessary. We shall look at these in more detail in the next chapter, but the main idea underlying web services is that they provide a means of making data available to other systems dynamically. For example, imagine that a tutor wants to access a student's assessment record while they are using the VLE. Instead of querying the copy of the data held within the VLE, it is held in the student records system only, and made available via a web services link within the VLE, so the tutor is accessing it direct from the student record system. From a user perspective there should be no difference in these approaches, but from an integration perspective there may be benefits in adopting one approach over another.

VLEs and library systems

The relationship between VLEs and library systems reflects the changes in practice and internal politics wrought by the advent of e-learning perhaps more than any of the other systems. There is a sense in which the very identity of libraries and their function in the educational process is at stake. Just as e-learning has induced much navel gazing and concern amongst educators regarding their role, and the potential commoditization of education, so it is with librarians. The answer, however, is largely the same – e-learning makes the store of information less significant, but in such an information-rich world it makes the skills of dealing with information more valuable.

One can view the potential new role of libraries on a continuum, from redundant to central. At one extreme the need for a library becomes superfluous – at its simplest this might be categorized as 'I've got Google, what do I need a library for?' At the other end of the continuum, we see libraries playing a much more pivotal and central role than they do currently in delivering (which involves finding, tagging and managing) diverse resources, which in effect constitute the core teaching material.

In VLE terms the redundant library model can be realized through the creation of specific learning resources and objects, which are stored in an

LCMS. In addition the course material makes use of articles that are available online, learning resources from freely accessible repositories, and so on. There is simply no need to interface with, or be aware of, a library.

In the library as central model, the content that the VLE delivers is mediated through the library, and may not be stored locally. In this scenario we could envisage a problem based approach, where an academic may set a number of tasks and, either through pre-selected resources or through library-enhanced search facilities, the students have to find sufficient information to complete those tasks. These resources will be in a variety of formats and types, including journal articles, websites, multimedia assets such as animation and video clips, blog entries, conference discussions, etc. By using federated search methods that can locate resources from a range of different databases, and suitable tagging and mark-up of those resources, then a wealth of information is made available. In between these two extremes are other scenarios whereby the library offers a variety of functions, such as helping educators identify resources, creating and maintaining collections, managing rights, etc. But in all these cases the nature of the library's role in relation to the student and the academic has been affected by the internet.

The VLE and library interface then is one fraught not only with problematic technical issues, but also with a political dimension. There have been no shortage of projects examining the interface between the two, indeed there is something of a project overload, without a real consensus being reached as to the ideal configuration. The main area where the two systems interface is with the location of resources, and more specifically the following:

- locating and importing resources into a VLE;
- storing data about new types of resources, for example learning objects, within library catalogues;
- managing rights and clearance for resources;
- indexing and describing resources.

In all these areas it is the provision of standards that is the key to success, and in this respect e-learning lags behind libraries, which have, of necessity, always adopted standards for cataloguing and describing materials. But libraries now have to deal with a wider range of materials; for instance describing video clips, or sections of video clips, so that they might be reused in course materials is a different problem from cataloguing books on shelves. E-learning changes the nature in which resources are used. One aspect of this is granularity, where someone may want a ten second clip from a fifteen minute resource. Another is that of context, for example a video segment about gang culture may contain some useful clips that show urban architecture, which could be used in a town-planning course, but the educator is unlikely to find these through a simple search.

In turn, educators have been developing standards to describe and package educational content so that it may be shared. The process now is one of bringing these two worlds together, so that a search in a library catalogue, using a library standard search protocol such as the Bath Profile, will reveal learning objects described according to an educational technology standard, say SCORM (Sharable Content Object Reference Model).

Feature annexing rears its head here also, with the LCMS being the main contender. Some LCMSs offer federated search, that is the ability to search across a number of databases and collections and treat those resources as if they were part of the central repository. In some institutions the LCMS will be part of the library's remit, and in others it will form part of the general IT provision, or be incorporated with the VLE, so there is the potential for duplication of function with library systems. Increasingly, however, it is not what the library holds that is significant, but rather what it locates. The library is probably best viewed as the gateway to the wider range of quality controlled resources, acting as both a broker and filter for the VLE.

Increasing the stock of metaphors

When asked what interest he could find in attending Sir Humphrey Davy's lectures, Samuel Coleridge responded, 'I attend Davy's lectures to increase my stock of metaphors.' Complex systems, such as MLEs, which are constituted from several sub-systems, themselves often a collection of functions and tools, require metaphors to help us understand systems for which there is no real evolutionary precedent. The stock of metaphors I would argue is rather lacking, and they carry a number of implicit assumptions which are never questioned. In this section I would like to extend our stock of metaphors, and highlight some of the assumptions in existing ones.

An MLE has a number of characteristics, which any metaphor should address and help us to understand:

- It is constituted from a range of separate systems which are largely autonomous.
- Data can be passed between these systems, but one system needs to be the 'owner' of that data.
- The sub-systems are owned by different groups who have different priorities and approaches.
- There will be a number of existing systems in place which are not likely to change significantly.
- There is a temporal dimension with some systems being phased out, others developing in functionality, and the needs of users altering over time.

I would argue that many of the current methods we have for describing MLEs do not capture some of these key characteristics and thus do not help us in establishing a vision for an MLE that can be shared by all.

The common method of articulating the interactions in these highly complex systems is to use architectural diagrams. Even the term 'architecture' carries with it connotations, for instance, that there are rigid walls, a solid structure, sub-division into smaller units, construction according to sound engineering principles, etc. Consider how different our expectations would be, but perhaps equally appropriate, if we were to talk of a systems soup or organism even. For a soup it might suggest that the components are blended together and there is a predefined algorithm (recipe) for its creation, whereas for an organism one might suppose a complex interaction of different subsystems, an evolutionary history, a measure of some overall 'health' and so on. Most architectural diagrams tend to suggest that systems have 'hard' edges, whereas in reality these boundaries tend to be much fuzzier. Feature annexing means that there is a constant bleed between systems.

Another common metaphor is that of a jigsaw puzzle, with each piece fitting neatly into predefined spaces, locking into position with carefully constructed interfaces, each element bound by hard edges, and combining to create a cohesive whole. However, as we have seen in this chapter, many of these assumptions are not true of MLEs, and probably not true of all hybrid, institutional systems. There are some areas where the jigsaw metaphor breaks down – for instance the overlap in functions between systems, and also the ability to add a new system for a previously unidentified need, such as e-portfolios do not fit with the model of a jigsaw which, once completed, has no room for extension. Given the continually evolving nature of hybrid systems, this seems like a serious limitation on the metaphor. Another limitation on the jigsaw view is that it does not reflect the autonomy of the components found in hybrid systems such as MLEs. A jigsaw piece does not have meaning by itself, it only makes sense as part of a whole, whereas many of the subsystems in an MLE can exist as independent systems, for instance one could run the library system separately from the VLE.

It might be better to think of such complex systems as inflatables within a temporarily confined space, like a box full of balloons, so as one expands it does so at the expense of another. As new functions are required that are not provided by any current systems, the total functional space is effectively expanded to accommodate this new system. But this metaphor does not really address the issue of systems taking over the function of others, and of information flow between the systems.

Another metaphor might be more organic in nature, where we view the systems as a culture of micro-organisms. Given the manner in which hybrid systems evolve over time, with legacy systems becoming integrated into newer systems, there is some appeal to the organic view. One might imagine systems as being essentially phagocytic in nature, seeking to engulf others as they take on their functionality, and other systems resisting this in the same manner that pathogens resist phagocytes in the blood, such as by occupying areas where phagocytes do not go, so with systems that would entail specializing in functionality that the larger system(s) will not replicate. This metaphor is different from many others which suggest cooperation, where this is essentially competitive. This may in fact reflect the reality more closely, as manufacturers and developers seek to expand the feature set of their products thus increasing their value and position within a hybrid set-up. Although they have a core function, each system is essentially seeking to engulf the role of other systems, and thus increase the chances of its own survival.

I am not suggesting that any of these metaphors are superior to existing ones, but by using different metaphors, just as with the use of scenarios, we can think about how these systems operate and develop in different ways. We should not allow our models to be constrained by a set of metaphors which were developed for one environment, but which may no longer apply as needs and technology change.

Conclusion

In this chapter we have looked at how various systems need to interact with a VLE, in order to create a functional MLE. With each system the technical issues are only one dimension of the problem. The range of systems that the VLE needs to interact with demonstrates that it has an impact across all university functions and areas. The introduction of a new system such as a VLE creates a reaction in each of these areas also, as adjustments are made to working practice, and also the future implications for the role of people in that area are debated. We have seen how feature annexation means that the separate systems in an MLE can expand and contract, and the anxiety is that a similar process occurs with the various departments who are responsible for those systems. When we talk about the integration of a VLE into a wider MLE we usually mean integration in the limited technical sense, but integration in a political and cultural sense is probably more significant. This chapter has sought to highlight that the boundaries between systems are not as well defined as is often supposed, and thus delineating these boundaries is a matter of choice, which should be shaped by an understanding of their impacts upon learners and staff.

Chapter 7

Standards and specifications

One of the consequences of the internet is that it accelerates the need for a solution to problems that have often been around for some time. One such problem in education and training has been interoperability between institutions. Throughout this book I have made reference to a number of educational technology and technical standards that have a direct bearing on VLEs. The rise in VLEs has been linked with the development of many of these standards and specifications, primarily because the need for interoperability became evident to developers and users. Interoperability is at the heart of most standards; for example by standardizing the design of plugs and plug sockets we make them interoperable with all electrical devices, and do not have the situation where I have one plug for Sony devices, another for those made by Samsung, and so on. This type of proprietary situation was developing in e-learning (and some would argue it is still the case), so that content created for one VLE could not easily be deployed in another. Problems with interoperability existed prior to the rise of the internet, but it is with e-learning that the need to find solutions to them has gained momentum. So, while previously learning resources may have been exchanged in the format of books, articles, slides or software files, there is now a move to create digital resources that can be reused in the form of learning objects. Similarly, students have always moved between institutions, but the internet makes organizations more permeable and likely to enter into partnerships, so students may take courses from more than one place, or an institution may have an agreement with another one to share courses. In this case having student record systems that all operate in a different, proprietary manner makes the exchange of data difficult. By specifying open standards, that are not owned by one company, all institutions can adopt these and the exchange of resources, data, and services is simplified. As we saw in the previous chapter, there are a number of systems that a VLE needs to interface with, and so specifying standard formats for the exchange of data between these systems would potentially ease the implementation of VLEs.

The main areas of concern for interoperability are:

- the exchange of learning resources;
- the passing of data between institutions (such as student records);
- the interoperability of software on more than one platform;
- the ability for software applications to communicate with other systems.

More recently there has been a focus on the reuse of learning activities, which has given rise to the Learning Design specification. This has particular interest for educators, and so will be treated separately in the next chapter, although it is one of the suite of specifications developed by IMS amongst others.

In addition there have been some developments in broader technical standards that have implications for educational systems. Web services, which provide a means of loose enterprise integration without the need for extensive (and expensive) reengineering of existing systems, are the most prominent of these and so will be considered in this chapter. A related area of interest is the work on open source projects, such as Sakai in the US, which have interoperability as a key aim. One of the benefits of these approaches is the development of standards for describing various tools and services, so these can be swapped in and out. We will look at the open source world in Chapter 9.

Web services

The idea behind web services is that a piece of code is available to remote machines over the internet. The code in effect acts as a service, providing functionality or data to a remote machine without having to download the code. It is delivered over the web (or more accurately the internet), hence the term web services. Muschamp (2004: 10) defines them as 'services that can communicate with other services over a network, using a set of standard technologies'. He suggests that in order for this to happen, a number of key objectives must be met.

The technologies must be:

- platform agnostic – infrastructure from all vendors must support the same specifications;
- language agnostic – a service written in one language must implement the specifications for web services in the same way as that written in a different language;
- free from restrictive intellectual property rights (IPR) terms – that is, the developers of the technologies must have widespread adoption as their primary goal.

To meet these basic objectives three standards have been developed which define web services:

- SOAP (Simple Object Access Protocol) – this is a protocol for message exchange so one system knows how to communicate with another.
- UDDI (Universal Description, Discovery and Integration) – web services are stored in a registry, where a subscriber can find the web service they are looking for. This directory is described by UDDI.
- WSDL (Web Services Description Language) – there needs to be a standard way of describing web services, so that they can be located. Example fields would include the name, any parameters that must be passed to it and the nature of the response. The UDDI directory is therefore constituted from pointers to WSDL files which describe particular services.

XML (Extensible Markup Language) underpins all of this and is at the heart of web services, being the method by which data is packaged and passed between systems. As mentioned above web services are language-agnostic, thus one developer might use Java to develop its service, and another use Visual Basic, but they could still communicate through SOAP (as long as the languages can accept XML input). This is significant because it means services can be integrated across different systems without the need for costly reengineering of both systems (although the implementation of web services will have an associated cost).

Web services can be thought of as a relationship between a provider and consumer. The service can take the form of functionality or access to data. The motivation for adopting web services is that they avoid duplication of functionality and data – these only need be created once and then made available via web services to all packages that may require them.

Web services are often promoted as a solution to the integration of several institutional systems. Their advantage in this area is that they do not require expensive integration of databases or recoding of existing systems. They are simpler, based on open standards (and not proprietary solutions), more flexible and cheaper than many of the alternative integration methods. Hansen *et al.* (2003: 176) claim that 'many of these complex integration tasks can now be reduced to defining XML interfaces between an aggregator and an aggregated system. In addition, reusability will be improved, because once a Web Services interface is developed, it can be used by multiple integrators.'

As we saw in the last chapter the VLE poses a number of integration problems, and web services offer one method of overcoming these across most applications, without the need for extensive alteration to existing systems. Perhaps the most significant contribution of the web services approach is that it renders the boundaries of systems much more permeable. A direct, almost hardwired, integration with each system is not required, but instead the various services a system can offer are opened up and made available. In order to expose these software components, a service oriented architecture is required. Thus the concept of a VLE built around such an architecture, which we have touched upon in previous chapters and will look at in more detail in Chapter 9, has been developed partly on the basis of the web services methodology.

However, as with all technological solutions, there are drawbacks and a web services approach is not always suitable. Hansen *et al.* (2003) provide the following list of potential difficulties with a web services approach:

- Semantics – the semantic description that can be realized in web services is limited, and different services may attach different names to the same type of data, or give the same name to different types of service. Davies *et al.* (2004: 121) suggest that the Semantic Web initiative, which seeks to provide rich semantic data about online resources, as a means of overcoming this, suggesting that 'the use of Semantic Web technology in describing web services more fully and formally offers the possibility of being able to compose, in a fully automated way, a set of web services to achieve a specific user requirement'.
- Modularization of business processes – just as the advent of the internet has seen an increase in modularization in many industries (consider the success of iTunes) and in education (as witnessed by the advent of learning objects), so the web service approach demands that business processes be broken up into smaller, discrete elements that can be accessed for one specific function. Both technically and operationally many business processes are not easily modularized in this fashion, and as with the learning object approach, there may be resistance to working this way.
- Security and trusted intermediaries – I mentioned above that web services make systems more permeable, which is useful when integrating systems, but potentially dangerous when exposing data and functionality to a range of other systems and users. Therefore methods for ensuring the security of a system are required. From a user's perspective they similarly need to be able to trust the information they provide will not be misused.
- Quality and source selection – as the number of web services grows, the problem of knowing how to trust the information gained through such systems increases. A web service could still be active, for example, but the data it provides is outdated, and the user would have no way of detecting this. If web services operate internally within an organization this is less of an issue, but as they expand in general use then knowing how to select the most appropriate and reliable source becomes an issue.
- Licensing and payment mechanisms – again, if web services are adopted as a method of integrating internal systems then this not an issue, but external companies may make data and services available via web services, in which case payment methods need to be developed.
- Development tools – as with all new developments, creating the appropriate tool set is a prime factor in their adoption.

To this list we could also add that of efficiency. If we consider a complex network, with many different web services available, then it is possible to envisage a situation where the call to one web service necessitates a call to another, and so on, with complex and recursive data passing, location of services and negotiation between systems required to complete the task. As the number of web services increases, predicting the possible combinations of different services and estimating the load on systems becomes difficult and thus comparisons in terms of efficiency with other methods of integration are necessary.

Learning technology standards

E-learning in general, and VLEs in particular, raise a number of interoperability issues for organizations, which can be summarized as:

- integrating and linking the VLE with existing systems within the organization;
- incorporating materials from other providers within the VLE;
- sharing student data with other institutions;
- defining standard operations and data sets for a range of software tools;
- specifying the learner's pathway through resources.

In the international educational field, these issues have crystallized around the specification of interoperability standards and specifications for e-learning materials through the work of bodies such as IMS and Advanced Distributed Learning (ADL).

The key specifications can be placed in categories according to their core function:

- Specifications used to describe, discover and exchange content. These include:
    - Metadata – a structured way to associate descriptive information with content to facilitate search and delivery;
    - Content Packaging – facilitates interchange of content between different learning systems by providing a way to package learning information and meta-data;
    - Question & Test Interoperability (QTI) – provides a structure for the description and packaging of assessments and questions. Also provides a results reporting mechanism;
    - Digital Repositories Interoperability – provides recommendations for the interoperation of the most common repository functions such as searching or submitting content.

- Specifications for content interaction and tracking. These include:
  - Simple Sequencing – defines a method for sequencing discrete learning activities using rules that describe the branching or flow of instruction according to the outcomes of a learner's interactions with content;
  - Competencies – defines a model for representing and tracking competencies associated with content and learners;
  - Learning Design – provides a framework and a language for describing the design of learning experiences and to share that design between systems;
  - Accessibility – provides guidelines for developing user interfaces and content that are accessible to learners using alternative access systems.
- Specifications for application system interoperability include:
  - Learner Information Package (LIP) – provides a structure for organizing learner information for sharing across learning environments and administrative systems;
  - Enterprise – facilitates the transfer of organizational information about students and learning groups between application systems.

We will now look at the most significant of these standards and how they relate to VLEs.

Metadata

Metadata often seems to be something of an obsession of those working in the educational standards field. There seems to be no problem that cannot potentially be resolved by the addition of another field in the resource's metadata. There is a tendency to bury even the smallest resource beneath a catalogue of metadata. While metadata is important, particularly for non-textual resources that cannot be searched easily, the effort in creating metadata means that elaborate requirements are unlikely to be satisfied. It is also far from clear that large metadata sets are useful; in short, more is not necessarily better.

One of the main motivations for extensive metadata tagging is that it will help the *automatic* aggregation of content, so computers can select and assemble resources on the fly, creating a course for just-in-time delivery. My suspicion is that such automatic selection and aggregation will only work in very procedural domains, and probably not at higher education level. Thus if we remove this requirement from metadata, and assume that there will be some human intervention in the selection and aggregation of resources, then the metadata set we need to find, assess and ensure intellectual property rights becomes considerably smaller.

Another area of metadata that I remain unconvinced about is that of secondary, or usage, data, whereby the context in which the resource has been, or could be, used is described. First, it is almost impossible to predict all the contexts in which a resource might be used, and second if we assume human intervention is occurring then that person is the best judge as to the suitability of that resource in their context.

One of the issues surrounding metadata is the effort required to create it. Often the people best suited to doing so are the authors, but having created a learning object, say, an academic is often disinclined to spend further time inputting metadata into a series of forms. A good deal of metadata can be generated automatically, for instance the format, date of creation, copyright, author, etc can all be gathered from systems that store the resources, such as an institutional LCMS. As the Automatic Metadata Generation (2006) project website states, 'we cannot (solely) rely on humans for metadata creation: humans "don't scale" and humans are not perfect. More importantly, producing metadata is not exactly fun!' However, there are some elements of metadata, for example estimated study time, that cannot be harvested automatically (although again one should ask the question how important that type of information is to anyone seeking to find a resource).

The IEEE Learning Object Metadata (LOM) is one standard for specifying metadata which has been widely accepted in the US. In the UK this has been used as the base for the UK LOM Core (2004), which aims to set out a core number of metadata fields for educational content. This has been broadly accepted as a standard for educational markup in the UK now. Similarly, in Canada there is CanCore, and in Australia the EdNA Metadata Standard, with variations and local adaptations available in most countries.

The UK LOM Core has three levels of optionality for its fields:

- Mandatory – these elements must be completed in order for an object to be recognized as UK LOM Core valid.
- Optional – these elements may be completed.
- Optional (recommended) – these elements should be completed where possible.

With over twenty elements for each of these three categories, the UK LOM Core is still a considerable set of data. The UK LOM Core groups the elements into nine distinct categories:

- General – these describe the learning object overall.
- Life cycle – these elements describe the history and current state of the learning object and those who have affected it.
- Meta-metadata – describes the metadata record itself, rather than the learning object.

- Technical – describes the technical requirements and characteristics of the object.
- Educational – describes the key educational or pedagogic characteristics of the learning object.
- Rights – describes the intellectual property rights and conditions of use.
- Relation – defines the relationship between the learning object and other learning objects, if any.
- Annotation – this category provides comments on the educational use of this learning object, and information on when and by whom the comments were created.
- Classification – this category describes where this learning object falls within a particular classification system.

Content Packaging

Being able to swap contents between VLEs and retain their structure was an early priority for standardization. The minimum requirement here is that you should be able to take a set of resources linked together in sequence so that they form a course, and transfer it from VLE A to VLE B without needing to modify the resources or recreate the structure. The IMS Content Package Specification (IMS 2005b) does allow you to do this. As the best practice guide states, its aim is to define 'interoperability between systems that wish to import, export, aggregate, and disaggregate packages of content'. However, one of the criticisms of Content Packaging is that this is achieved only at a rather simplistic level.

Content Packaging represents both the success and problems of the educational technology standards movement. It has been successful in establishing a standard that is commonly recognized and used so, in comparison with many of the other standards, Content Packaging has a high level of adoption. However, in order to accommodate the wide variety of systems and resources, the specification has become so generic as to almost become meaningless. Simply putting an IMS Content Package wrapper around some content is sufficient for it to become compliant with the specification. This is sufficient if all you wish to do is have a set of resources set out in a linear fashion, but when you create courses that require interaction with a number of tools, for example using a forum for a debate and a voting tool, then interoperability begins to break down, as the calls to these tools are specific to the particular VLE.

Content Packaging has attempted to overcome this problem by acting as an *uber* specification, which can include a number of other specifications. For example, Learning Design packages are specified within a Content Package, and thus more complex designs, complete with calls to different services, can be accommodated in this manner. However, as we shall examine later, creating generic descriptions of a service, so that any forum system, say, can be called from within the system is far from trivial.

These criticisms aside, this specification represents the bare minimum for any form of interoperability and any VLE and LCMS that feeds it must be able to present material delivered in this format and export material in this format to other systems. Initially there was mixed success in importing and exporting packages between systems, despite the claims of manufacturers (for example Boyle 2002). More recently interoperability has been demonstrated in most major packages (see http://www.reload.ac.uk/interop.html for some examples). The success of Content Packaging is that it is relatively simple for educators to use, and does not require a detailed understanding of the specification or XML to create a standard compliant package. This is aided by a number of tools, for example most LCMS systems will allow you to collect a set of resources together and publish these as an IMS Content Package, and editors such as Reload (http://www.reload.ac.uk/) offer easy to use tools for individuals.

Question & Test

The IMS Question & Test Interoperability (QTI) Specification (IMS 2006a) provides a standard XML language for describing questions and tests. After the exchange of content, being able to exchange assessment was the next highest priority for the standards movement, as assessment sits at the heart of the educational process, and also because one of the primary benefits of VLEs is their ability to provide formative assessment throughout a course. There is good evidence that formative assessment improves learning (see Black and Wiliam 1998), with feedback helping students identify gaps in their current understanding and providing remedial action (Sadler 1989). It therefore represents one of the strong selling points of VLEs, and thus an area likely to attract the attention of the standards bodies.

Initially this centred on specifying standard formats for multiple choice questions (MCQs). This left the standard, and by extension all educational technology standards and VLEs, open to the accusation that they were both overly restrictive and lacked an understanding of higher educational needs. While MCQs represent the majority of online assessments, they are often seen as rather limited in their educational benefit, as they tend to promote rote learning, provide students with choices and thus do not replicate usual practice and are pedagogically unsound. The accusation of restriction was somewhat misguided, since it misunderstood the role of standards – they do not preclude any form of extension, but instead provide a base level. More recent question specifications, including IMS QTI v2, have a much more extensive range of question types. QTI v2 has six categories of question type:

- Simple items – these cover the main forms of automatic assessment, including multiple choice, matching responses, simple text entry, missing words, clicking on hot spots in an image and positioning an object.

- Composite items – these can mix or have multiple instances of the same interaction, thus allowing sequences of questions.
- Response processing – these use a general response processing language, of the if–then–else variety, to allow more complex responses and feedback.
- Feedback – this item is based on the result of response processing. There are two types, modal (shown after response) and integrated (shown during subsequent attempts and embedded into the text).
- Adaptive – these allow an item to be scored adaptively over a number of attempts, so for instance a student can be given different questions based on their responses.
- Item templates – these can specify similar items, so the same type of question can be reused with different variables.

This represents more than most educators are likely to realize, and so accusations of restriction arising from the standards are less justifiable now. However, the use of a processing language means that the items become complex, and the benefit gained through the use of simple tools such as those found in VLEs is lost. This represents the fundamental dilemma for all educational technology standards – if they are to be adopted they need to be simple to use, even invisible, since they can be accomplished through tools that most educators can use, and yet if they are to sufficiently capture the complexity of the educational process, particularly in higher education, then they require a level of sophistication and density that make them unusable by most educators.

The real benefit in adopting a standard for automatic assessment is the ability to create banks of question items. This has two main advantages:

1 It extends the range of questions and alleviates the burden of writing them. Creating questions that are varied and require thought on behalf of the student is not an easy, or very enjoyable, task. By creating banks of questions that can be imported into any VLE, the writing process can be shared by a greater number of educators, and even outsourced to third parties to write the questions. In the same way that a learning object approach can lower the cost and increase the quality of e-learning resources, so question banks can create a distributed network for the creation of question items. However, as with learning object repositories, getting a critical mass of contributions is key to the success of such an approach.
2 It facilitates adaptive questioning and variation in testing. By creating tests from a random selection of questions from a sufficiently large pool of items, then students can be retested on the same topic without receiving the same test twice. Similarly students in the same cohort will receive different tests, thus reducing the likelihood of exchanging answers. A large bank of question items that are appropriately tagged can be used

for adaptive questioning, for example if a student shows a particular area of misunderstanding they can be given more questions relating to that specific subject, or students who score well can be provided with more advanced questions.

Simple Sequencing

This specification provides a way of describing sequencing of learning activities, so that learners can progress along a pathway through material, which is influenced by their behaviour. As its name suggests, it is not aimed at addressing some of the more complex types of sequencing that may occur, and is deliberately limited in scope. It seeks to specify how directed, self-guided and some adaptive sequencing can be interpreted by a VLE. Collaborative activities are outside the scope of the specification; these can be accommodated within the Learning Design specification (see Chapter 8). The practical application of Simple Sequencing is to attach assessment to some of the resources, and then describe pathways that are dependent on the outcome of these. For example a pass in one assessment may cause resource X to be revealed, while a fail reveals resource Y.

The prescribed nature of this process, and the lack of any provision for collaborative activities, has led many in higher education to dismiss Simple Sequencing as unsuitable, and applicable to training only. This view is enhanced by the use of Simple Sequencing in the SCORM profile, which is aimed at more training purposes and supported by the US Ministry of Defense. Attempting to define the possible pathways and interactions that occur during complex learning is either too problematic or would produce a program of such size and complexity as to be unwieldy. In the Simple Sequencing best practice guide (IMS 2003a) a simple example of using the package Photoshop runs to several pages of XML code just to describe the interactions, without the actual resources. This is a highly structured domain, and so attempting to create a sequence for a course in 'Understanding Middle Eastern politics', say, would be arduous to say the least.

This is not to suggest that Simple Sequencing is without its uses in higher education, however, and in reality it was never intended to address the sort of interactions that would take place in the sort of course mentioned above. For example, courses with large cohorts could benefit from having a number of simple sequences around major topics, in addition to the human-mediated support and dialogue. With a large number of students the initial investment would be worthwhile and the varied needs could be accommodated. Similarly preparatory material could be presented through a structured sequence, so students could start any course with a common base level of knowledge, without the need for support prior to the course start.

There is an associated cost with Simple Sequencing, in creating the sequence itself which requires both technical expertise, but also knowledge elicitation from the educator to establish the appropriate pathway. It is also necessary to create, or adapt, resources to an appropriate format, so they are of a suitable modularity and make use of assessment. Another issue which Simple Sequencing raises is the overlap between specifications, whereby the same objective can be reached via a number of different routes. Just as we saw feature annexation in systems, so there seems to be a degree of cross-over between the specifications. For example, if we wish to give users different resources or information based on their performance, this can be achieved through Simple Sequencing, Learning Design, QTI, or some combination of these.

Other specifications

The specifications discussed above represent the most significant ones for most educators. There are many more specifications that have been, or are in the process of being, developed that will have bearing on a VLE. A selection of these is summarized below:

- Accessibility – this specification refers to more than just commonly defined accessibility issues. It defines a means to specify accessibility preferences and learner accommodations. These preferences go beyond support for disabled people to include kinds of accessibility needs such as mobile computing, noisy environments, etc.
- Learning Information Package – this specifies a collection of information about a learner (individual or group learners) or a producer of learning content (creators, providers or vendors). The core structures of the IMS LIP are based upon: accessibilities; activities; affiliations; competencies; goals; identifications; interests; qualifications, certifications and licences; relationship; security keys; and transcripts.
- Enterprise – the scope of the IMS Enterprise Specification is focused on defining interoperability between systems residing within the same enterprise or organization. It is intended to support interoperability between VLEs and the following classes of Enterprise systems:

    - human resource systems
    - student administration systems
    - training administration systems
    - library management systems.

- E-portfolio – this will enable the portability of e-portfolios between e-portfolio tools and systems using existing specifications and standards. This is particularly important for e-portfolios which are seen as residing with the individual, and so can be used throughout that individual's learning experience across multiple institutions.

- General Web Services – this effort is defining web service technology standards that will be used across all IMS specifications. It will include a base profile of core web service technologies as well as best practice guidance on issues such as webservice security and routing. As such it demonstrates the extent to which web services have become the means by which the specifications are implemented.
- Reading List Interoperability – this effort is defining a specification for the interoperability of resource lists (such as reading lists) between library information management systems and e-learning systems, such as course management systems. It is defining the data and web services for exchanging the data.

Conclusion

As someone who has fitfully tried to promote standards I have some sympathy with the ethnographer in Perec's *Life: A user's manual* (1978: 112), who discovered an obscure tribe and offered them an array of gifts and knowledge. He was perplexed as to why they would abandon their village for no reason and move to increasingly uninhabitable locations, until he realized that

> they had no use whatever for the gifts I laid beside them, no use at all for the help I thought I could give! It was because of me that they abandoned their villages and it was only to discourage me, to convince me there was no point in my persevering that they chose increasingly inhospitable sites, imposing ever more terrible living conditions on themselves to show me they would rather face tigers and volcanoes . . .

The area of standards often feels like one where an awful amount of energy is being expended on creating carefully worded and formulated specifications that no-one really wants or needs. Like Perec's tribe, most academics have no use for these gifts. In this section we will look at two reasons why the uptake of specifications has not been as widespread as might have been predicted.

The first question to ask is why is there all this effort and expenditure in developing them? The main reason is that interoperability is such a desirable goal, and seems to meet so many needs in e-learning. But often these are solutions to anticipated problems in creating a future which is deemed desirable by those working in this field. It may not be acknowledged very often but there are implicit political or economical assumptions underlying much of the standardization work. It is assumed, for instance, that lifelong learning will become more significant, with a focus on the individual. If one accepts this assumption, then the need for an e-portfolio standard that allows users to migrate between institutions seems like a logical, and inevitable, outcome. The assumption of a more learner-centric view of the organizational process in education is far from unproblematic (I am not referring to particular pedagogies here, but rather how we configure educational systems, which are currently structured around institutions). One could make similar arguments for any of the standards, for example the whole notion of reusable content has a large set of assumptions and implications, which were listed in the section on LCMSs, and which are controversial for many educators.

This contextual myopia which seems to afflict many in the standards world means they may not be addressing the main issues. There is an unspoken belief that if we create the standards, they will come, but this is to ignore or at least underestimate the concomitant changes in academic culture that each of the standards assumes.

Another problem with the overall acceptance of standards is one that I raised with regards to QTI, and which we might term the 'complexity paradox'. If they are to be useful then they need to capture the sophistication in much of the educational process and related technologies, but in order to do so they soon reach the stage where only experts can understand them. As I suggested in Chapter 1, common VLE tools have helped bring the educator back into close proximity with the technology, without the need for intermediaries. I feel that this proximity is the key to success for any technology, and if we look at the list of popular technologies in Chapter 4, they all possess this democratizing quality. The introduction of complex standards goes against this trend, and potentially introduces a further layer between the educator and the learning experience they wish to create. There are three possible solutions to this (if we accept that the extremes of abandoning the whole educational technology approach or making all educators experts in educational technology are not viable options):

- Employ expert educational technologists to act as intermediaries between educators and the technologies.
- Create smarter tools that allow educators to work with the specifications without requiring detailed knowledge of them.
- Adopt a hybrid approach where simpler tools are used directly by educators in the creation of their material, while more complicated items involve specialist educational technologists.

The conclusion to all this is that a wide range of standards and specifications is in existence, which have varied success and are at different stages of development. While the underlying assumption of increased interoperability is probably both desirable and inevitable, the political and cultural assumptions that it embodies will prove far more difficult to overcome than the technical challenges.

Chapter 8

Learning Design

Learning Design is the specification that interests most educators, largely because unlike some of the more technical ones, it actually seems to be about education. So what is Learning Design? It aims to provide a framework for describing teaching strategies and learning objectives in a method that allows easy interchange between e-learning providers. It is based on the Educational Modelling Language (EML) developed at the Open University of the Netherlands (Hummel *et al.* 2004).

There is some confusion surrounding the term, since it has become popular as an expression that in a more general sense is synonymous with instructional or course design. For example someone might ask, 'What is the learning design underlying this course?' They do not expect to be presented with XML code when they ask this, but are seeking some rationale behind the course design, for example an explanation that relates learning outcomes to pedagogy and content. This extension of the term partly reflects the interest the specification has generated. In order to distinguish between this more general use of the term and reference to the IMS specification itself Britain (2004) suggests the 'convention of using "learning design" (small "l", small "d") when we are talking about the general concept and "Learning Design" (Capital "L" and "D") when referring to the concept as implemented in the IMS specification'.

The IMS Learning Design is based on the analogy of a play, with roles and acts. The *IMS Learning Design Best Practice and Implementation Guide* (IMS 2003b) states that

> the core concept of the Learning Design Specification, is that regardless of pedagogical approach, a *person* gets a *role* in the teaching–learning process, typically a *learner* or a *staff* role. In this role he or she works toward certain *outcomes* by performing more or less structured *learning* and/or *support activities* within an *environment*. The environment consists of the appropriate *learning objects and services* to be used during the performance of the activities. Which role gets which activities at what moment in the process, is determined by the *method* or by a *notification*.

It thus aims to be descriptive, or expressive, not prescriptive, and applicable to all pedagogical approaches. While this is true, there is an implicit assumption in LD that an activity-based approach is beneficial. It does not exclude a more passive content-driven model, but rather there is little to be gained from using the LD approach if you simply wish to sequence some content, as other specifications (content packaging and simple sequencing) can achieve this more easily.

There are three levels of Learning Design:

- Level A – this is the simplest form and covers the activities, roles, acts and environment used in a Learning Design.
- Level B – this introduces the notion of properties and conditions. It is at this level that LD becomes useful, as it allows what-if conditions and storing properties (such as student performance) to allow for multiple paths through learning material.
- Level C – this supports notification or messaging between system components, which allows for a more dynamic workflow and personalization.

At an institutional or individual level, there are several reasons why adopting Learning Design may be beneficial:

1 It provides a means by which learning designs can be reused and shared, compared with just sharing content.
2 It can act as a means of eliciting designs from academics in a format that can be tested, and reviewed with technical and support staff.
3 It creates an audit trail of academic design decisions.
4 It aids learners in complex activities by guiding them through the activity sequence.

For benefits 2 and 3, the adoption of Learning Design could only be partial, so that although it is used to elicit and record course design decisions, the final course delivery is not in a Learning Design format.

Creating a Learning Design

There are three steps to creating a Learning Design, which we will examine with a simple example. The steps are:

1 Devise a use case narrative. This involves describing the problem in terms of a narrative, according to a predefined template.
2 Create a UML diagram. UML (Unified Modelling Language) is a method for depicting activities in a manner which is independent of the particular implementation. The technique is used widely in software development

as a method for defining features and gaining consensus between users and developers.

3 Develop XML code. The UML diagram then forms the basis for creating the XML document that implements the Learning Design.

We will look at each of these steps now, using an example called 'Technology viewpoints' (see Appendix, page 165). This is quite a simple example as it contains just two activities which are conducted in linear sequence, and there is no interaction with other students, so it only focuses on the individual learner. It would correspond to Level A in the Learning Design specification. For our purposes, however, a simple example is adequate to demonstrate the process.

Step 1: Use case narrative

The first step in the design phase is to produce a *use case narrative.* The components of this are specified as:

Title – a very short description.
Narrative – a general description of the use case in educational terms (see below).
Primary actor – student in student led learning, teacher in teacher led situations.
Scope – runtime systems involved in the delivery.
Level – description of the level of complexity.
Stakeholders and interests – a discussion of the roles and their respective responsibilities.
Preconditions – a specification of what is needed in order to provide the student with learning experiences.
Minimal guarantees – role specific preconditions.
Success guarantees – role specific demands for the learning experience to be successful.
Main success scenario – relate to the runtime systems involved.
Extensions – various failure scenarios.

We can complete this for the example content as follows:

Title – technology viewpoints.
Narrative – (see below).
Primary actor – student.
Scope – web server.
Level – masters.
Stakeholders and interests – independent study for students, may feed into student forums.

Preconditions – none.
Minimal guarantees – none.
Success guarantees – Successful completion of two grids.
Main success scenario – grids submitted to portfolio.
Extensions – none.

The narrative element of the use case narrative is specified as having the following components:

Title – a very short description.
Provided by – author, institution, etc.
Pedagogy/type of learning – case-based, problem-based, individualized linear, etc.
Description/context – a brief description of the design.
Learning objectives – the stated learning objectives of the design.
Roles – the various participants, such as student, tutor, assessor, etc.
Different types of learning content used – local texts, internet pages, multimedia DVDs.
Different types of learning services/facilities/tools used – external expert, groupware.
Different types of collaborative activities – among students, between students and tutors, etc.
Learning activity workflow – how actors/content/services interact.
Scenarios – for example the same content may be used for face-to-face and distance learning.
Other needs/specific requirements – for example accessibility, specific target groups, etc.

For the example this would be:

Title – Technology viewpoints.
Provided by – Martin Weller, The Open University.
Pedagogy/type of learning – Individualized linear.
Description/context – Technology viewpoints looks at the differing views of technology, focusing on technology and social determinism, and utopian and dystopian views. Relevant reading around these topics is provided. A grid is formed from these two continuums and students are required to place their own views on the internet on this grid. In activity two they do some more reading and place the views of the authors on the grid.
Learning objectives – An understanding of different viewpoints relating to technology. Experience in appreciating the viewpoints of authors.
Roles – Only one main role and actor: student.

Different types of learning content used – The following web content is used:

- Introduction
- Reading list (links to external articles)
- Activity 1 description
- Activity 2 description.

Different types of learning services/facilities/tools used – References Chapter 1 of the book Weller, M. (2002) *Delivering Learning on the Net: the why what and how of online education.* RoutledgeFalmer.
Different types of collaborative activities – None.
Learning activity workflow – There are four activities:

- Introduction
- Reading
- Activity 1
- Activity 2

Scenarios – The same content may be used for face-to-face and distance learning.
Other needs/specific requirements – None.

Step 2: UML activity diagram

The next step is to construct a UML activity diagram using the above narrative. According to the implementation guide, a 'UML activity diagrams place activities in a sequential or parallel order. Choices are allowed and activities may be nested. Also, responsibilities for activities may be indicated by the use of swim lanes.'

A diagram for the example content is shown in Figure 8.1. Note that I have made this sequential, so that Activity 2, for example, follows on from Activity 1. In Learning Design it is also possible to have alternative paths (or 'swim lanes'), so there could have been alternative strands, one with Activity 1 first (as above) and another with Activity 2 first.

Note also that as we are dealing with a single task, the granularity I have chosen is a single composite activity corresponding to the rectangular box. If we were to expand the LD to cover a course then there would be numerous activity structures i.e. multiple rectangles, nested within each other.

Step 3: The XML document instance

The next step is to create an XML document from the UML diagram. I won't provide the actual XML here (see http://sled.open.ac.uk/ and http://www.unfold-project.net/ for example Learning Designs), but instead I will set out the steps that need to be accomplished in creating the code.

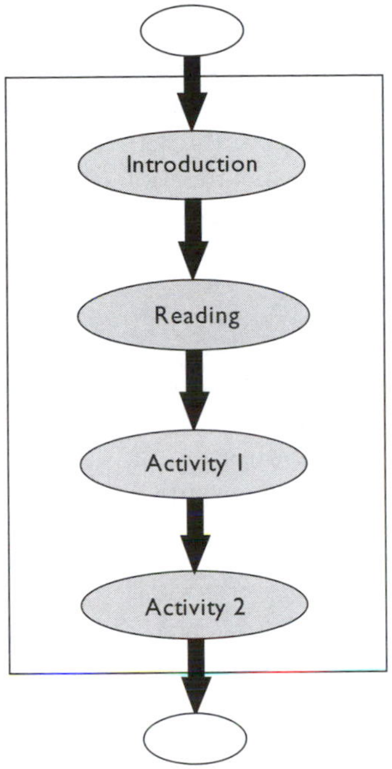

Figure 8.1 A Learning Design activity diagram.

1 Determine a title. The implementation guide advises that 'the title should reflect the kind of didactic scenario followed rather than the kind of content modelled with this particular scenario'. This will facilitate reuse of designs as well as content. So, for our example 'Single User Two Linear Activities' would suffice.

2 Add in components. There are four types of components: roles, properties, activities, and environments. In our case these are as follows:

- Roles – student.
- Properties – none (these are found in Level B).
- Activities – there is one activity structure (which corresponds to the object as a whole, the rectangular box in the diagram) and four learning activities (Introduction, Reading, Activity 1, Activity 2).
- Environment – this would be the environment or tools required (a web server in our case) but it could be a tool such as asynchronous discussion board.

3 Method. This is where the interactions are determined, using the analogy of a play, with acts and roles. In our simple case there is only one play, one act and one role. As the student studies individually here there is

no need for more than one role, but multiple roles can be used for collaborative tasks.

4 Link to content. The last step is to link the learning design to actual content. Note that Learning Design separates the learning design (the pedagogy) from the content. Both could be reusable elsewhere – for example, if you had created a Learning Design specification for an online debate with complex interactions, this could be reused with different content.

Learning Design tools

Having looked at the process of creating Learning Designs, your initial reaction might be that it is something of a sledgehammer to crack a nut. This is particularly true for simple examples and if you are doing the coding manually. What is required for Learning Design to be usable by non-experts are tools that hide much of the complexity in the specification. There are three types of tools relating to Learning Design:

1 Verifiers – these check that a Learning Design package conforms to the standard and highlight problems. Coppercore (http://coppercore.sourceforge.net/) from the Netherlands Open University is one tool for performing this (although it also does a lot more, acting as an 'engine' that handles the business logic of Learning Design, and can thus underpin other systems).
2 Authoring tools – these help developers create Learning Design packages. The Reload Learning Design editor (http://www.reload.ac.uk) is one such authoring tool.
3 Players – these run Learning Design packages, calling on the various tools required and presenting the resources as appropriate. The SLED (Service-based Learning Design System) player (http://sled.open.ac.uk) is an example of a system which handles the interface to the user, coordinating the various tools, and making calls to a Learning Design engine (Coppercore) to handle the various elements in a Learning Design package.

It may be that any one software package performs more than one of these functions, but these represent the main tasks that Learning Design software needs to accomplish. While all of these packages represent considerable advances in the use of Learning Design, they are not as easy to use as most commercial VLEs, and still require a knowledge of the Learning Design specification to use effectively.

The most successful Learning Design-type system is the Learning Activity Management System (LAMS), which we will look at in the next chapter. LAMS has inbuilt tools for the types of functions an educator might typically want to use, for example voting, discussion, etc. The other Learning Design tools listed here are more agnostic with regards to the actual services used. Part of the aim of Learning Design is that the designs themselves should be reusable. If they are linked to a specific software this limits their reuse potential, for example if an LD package had to use a particular tool found in Blackboard, say, then it would be unusable by anyone running a different VLE. Thus the success of the Learning Design approach is closely allied to the service-oriented approach. We will look at this in more detail in the next chapter, but for the purposes of this discussion we can think of a service-based approach as one that relies on generic descriptions of tools, so that any particular instance of a tool can be used, provided it complies with the general description. The reason Learning Design tools need this to be a reality is that without it, some of the benefits of Learning Design are lost. Earlier four potential reasons for adopting Learning Design were suggested, and without service-based approaches the potential for reuse is diminished and also the complexity that you can realize is reduced (corresponding to benefits 1 and 4 in the previous list). As we have seen, producing Learning Designs is a complex process, even with appropriate tools, and so the degree of investment required, in terms of understanding the approach, familiarizing yourself with the software, creating and then testing the Learning Designs, is only worthwhile if the Learning Designs are fairly complex themselves. Creating LDs similar to the one in the example does not represent a reasonable return on the investment required, since they are simple enough that they are unlikely to be reused, and from a student's perspective they do not need guidance. It is only when the task is relatively complex that the benefits of Learning Design are realized, and complex tasks are likely to require the use of a range of tools.

Issues in Learning Design

One of the main advantages of the Learning Design approach is reusability. So, while it may be complex and time-consuming to specify a design initially, once this has been done the *design* can be reused with different content. This is because Learning Design separates to some degree the content and the pedagogy. Within most institutions, the number of different types of activity is actually quite limited. Therefore a reasonably small set of Learning Designs could accommodate a large set of the institution's pedagogy. These can be assembled into many different types of course, with different content. What constitutes a reasonable pool of such designs is unknown, however, and as with content, many of the benefits of reuse are only realized once a critical mass has been achieved.

A potential concern about Learning Design might be the possibly prescriptive nature of each design. There may be events or paths that are unforeseen by the designer and an LD approach might not allow for the flexibility and dynamic nature in e-learning. LD does set out to be flexible but whether *any* specification can ever cover the type of interactions that take place in learning is an unresolved question and one that will probably only be solved by using LD in earnest.

Counter to this is the claim that LD aids the educator in specifying what it is they *want* to happen, and thus makes it more likely that their educational goals will be achieved. It is worth stressing that LD does not remove the human educator from the system, but because the specification has been made more explicit, it does mean that the environment can be used to aid the educator. For instance, many of the steps in a complex activity involving interactions between users and systems could be automated or at least have associated prompts. This is particularly important when operating on a large scale as it means a certain level of guidance can be assured.

The complexity paradox we encountered at the end of the last chapter is relevant to Learning Design also, in that in order for it to be useful it needs to address much of the complexity found in education, but by doing so it becomes incomprehensible to non-experts. The provision of good authoring tools can go a long way to overcoming this, but when a Learning Design is operating at levels B and C, which have prerequisites and conditions attached, this soon requires something akin to programming skills to realize.

Conclusion

The Learning Design specification was greeted with enthusiasm and a sense of relief from many in the educational technology field, as it was the first specification that seemed to address pedagogy, and in particular to countenance approaches such as collaboration. There was a feeling that although the other standards may be necessary, they were not going to generate a good deal of excitement amongst researchers and academics. Currently Learning Design stands on the cusp of moving beyond an interesting research area into more mainstream use. This is evidenced by the integration of Learning Design type tools and features into conventional VLEs such as Blackboard and Moodle. In such cases it may be that a Learning Design type tool is launched for a specific activity, without the whole course being represented as a Learning Design. There are some issues surrounding the complexity of the specification which may hinder its uptake. In the next chapter we will look at LAMS, which avoids some of these issues through the use of a visual interface and predefined activity structures. It may be that such tools, which incorporate the essence of a learning design approach without strictly adhering to the IMS specification, are the means by which reusable, structured activity sequences are realized.

For all the interest in Learning Design there is a fair deal of scepticism also. For instance, it resembles many similar attempts in the past to 'automate' the learning process, which have invariably faded after initial enthusiasm. The intelligent tutoring systems work that came out of the artificial intelligence field is one such example. While this fate may yet befall the Learning Design specification, I would suggest that three factors are converging which make a Learning Design type approach appealing. These factors are: the presence of VLEs which provide a technical platform which can be used as a springboard for Learning Design tools; the demand for e-learning with a resultant increase in audience; and growing interest from educators to do more than just deliver content.

Many of the technical problems we have discussed here overlap with those facing the open source community in general, and it is the tension between open source and commercial VLE options that we will look at in the next chapter.

Chapter 9

The open source option

In numerous places in this book we have touched upon the open source versus proprietary solution to VLEs, and we will explore this in detail in this chapter. 'Open source' can be seen as legal framework for the shared development and use of code, but it is also a set of shared beliefs about how code should be developed and who should own it. Any software can be developed for any purpose under an open source framework and a vast range is currently available. By contrast proprietary software is owned by the software producer and users pay a license fee to use it and crucially they do not have access to the source code (instead they have a compiled version) and so cannot see how the software works, or modify it. The principles of open source software and community have been well documented by Raymond (2001) and Weber (2004). Quoting Raymond, Stamelos *et al.* summarize it thus:

> The most known principles are 'release early and release often' and 'given enough eyeballs all bugs are shallow'. These two principles largely define the power of open source: (a) rapid evolution so that many users/programmers may be given the opportunity to use the new system and modify it, and no time is spent in 'unnecessary' management activities; and (b) many programmers working at the same time on the same problem, increasing the probability of its solution.
>
> (Stamelos 2002: 44)

The distinction in this chapter is between open source and proprietary software, and not open source and commercial because there are companies who offer open source software and support on a commercial basis, for example Red Hat sells the open source operating system Linux in a neatly packaged and installable version, along with associated support. The database system MySQL offers a dual licence for both open source and commercial partners. The company claims to have over 4,000 paying customers who have chosen the commercially licensed MySQL server, and yet have over 4 million users who use MySQL under the Gnu General Public License. Whilst technically there is only one product, the licences to use it are very different. The commercial licensees get support and an industrial strength application, which happens to come with a large developer base for new features, bug reports and testing. The open source licensees get a powerful system with no warranties or indemnification. Thus both parties can live harmoniously. This arrangement is something of a Holy Grail in open source terms, and is not the norm.

So, while proprietary is not exactly synonymous with commercial here, in many cases that may be a convenient way of thinking about the differences or, just as importantly, the *perceived* differences between the two approaches.

This may seem like primarily a technical debate, but the open source versus proprietary debate encapsulates many of the issues in e-learning, including:

- Pedagogy – it has been argued (for example by Kraan 2003a) that a single system cannot meet the various pedagogical needs of all subject communities. Thus a hybrid system with specialist tools for each subject area is desirable, which might favour a more service oriented, open source solution. However, this base assumption is debatable. It is flattering to feel that one's own subject area is somehow unique, and so it is a view that meets with a lot of support. If we look at the traditional campus university set-up then this wide variety of approaches is satisfied by some quite limited pedagogical environments and arrangements – the lecture, tutor group and laboratory meet most needs. Of course, what actually takes place in these broad containers varies considerably, but the same could be argued for a virtual environment, and as we saw in Chapter 3, a wide variety of pedagogical approaches can be accommodated within existing tools.
- Control and ownership – this would seem to favour an open source approach, since control is less in the hands of a commercial company, although there may be an individual or group who determine changes to the software in an open source approach, as is seen with Linux and Moodle. However, although one individual may be central, a community develops the software and any institution is free to adapt it to their needs, without being beholden to a commercial entity to make changes on their behalf. This is control and ownership in a technical sense; however, from an educator's perspective control is gained through ease of use. Commercial VLEs have focused on making this educator interface easy to use and thus passing some of the control back to the educator. Thus it might depend on how you define control and ownership as to which approach comes out most favourably.
- Commercialization – in general commercialization is seen as a negative influence in education, and something educators resist. Having a proprietary system at the heart of the learning experience would thus seem to be increasing the creep of commercialization into education. Those strongly opposed to this would generally favour an open source approach. However, education needs to operate in an increasingly competitive market, and is also more accountable with a range of procedures for

monitoring the quality of the student experience. Thus a proprietary system that needs to operate in such a commercial market may be better attuned to some of these needs.

- Robustness and reliability – proponents of the open source approach often point out that many of the most robust software applications in use today have come from an open source community, including Apache and Linux. It is less well acknowledged that many of the flakiest pieces of software come from this approach also. So while a successful open source project often surpasses proprietary solutions, those projects that operate on the fringes of people's time and do not create a large enough community often fall below the standard of proprietary solutions. One of the dangers inherent in the open source approach is that many projects are bound up with one individual, and when that individual moves on, or loses interest, then the project falters. The open source hub sourceforge.net is both a bustling community of vibrant projects and a graveyard of well intentioned software that has never quite gained sufficient momentum. While large projects such as VLEs may gain enough developers, the more specialist tools may not, or may not reach the level of robustness where they can be used by novices, and it is often on the provision of such tools that the open source model is promoted.

Open source approaches generally appear more favourable when they are compared on such criteria, although I have attempted to redress the balance somewhat. This is also reflected in the semantics that surrounds the two approaches. For instance, ask yourself what seems more appealing – community or company, gift culture or profit, shared or protected, altruism or greed? This is somewhat simplistic, but nevertheless the open source approach is surrounded by language and terminology that feels more comfortable and appealing, particularly to the higher education community.

One of the common fears, or misconceptions, about the open source approach is that the more mundane work will not be performed, since the developers are not paid for their contributions and recognition is the main reward. This might suggest that more exciting features would be of interest, while the more routine parts would be left unattended. This does not turn out to be the case, for instance Jorgensen (2001: 334) surveyed the contributors to the FreeBSD operating system and found that the 'project organizes a huge effort which is mainly of a maintenance-oriented nature. An approach likely to have contributed to a successful allocation of manpower to a type of work that might be perceived as boring or low status is the integration of bugfixing with new development.' Indeed Jorgensen suggests that the contrary may be true, and that the structure of the open source community (in this case at least) is best suited to this type of work, stating that the 'project's life cycle for changes may be, at least, insufficient as the basis for organizing work on complex new features' (Jorgensen 2001: 335).

Open source licensing

The critical distinguishing feature of open source development is that the entire source code of a project is vested in the public domain. The subsequent use of the publicly vested code is bound by licence.

The Free Software Foundation (2003) website provides a useful discussion of the range of these licences. The most common open-source licence is the Free Software Foundation's own General Public License from the Gnu project (GNU 1991). Under the GPL you can download and use the licensed software free of charge, regardless of how many people use it in your organization. However, if you modify the software and redistribute it, then under the Gnu GPL you are required to distribute the full source code of all that subsequent work as well.

There is also a vast range of alternative licence frameworks available to open source developments such as the BSD (Berkeley Software Distribution) and Creative Commons licence (http://creativecommons.org/).

Legally the major distinction between the types of licence in the open source community is related to the degree of insistence that all subsequent developments are also to be so vested in public. This is not always easy to enforce, for example if a small piece of open source code is used in much larger software, does it follow that the new software is also open source, leading to a degree of open source 'contagion'?

Educational open source

Although open source software such as Linux and Apache have been successful, and have been adopted by a number of higher educational establishments, open source developments for higher education have not been as prominent. The main focus in education had been in the K-12 market, largely in the US, and most projects have been on a small scale. However, over recent years this has begun to change and there are now a number of prominent open source projects. The reasons for this increased interest can be summarized as:

- *Financial* – as the cost of commercial software increases, and universities find themselves tied into increasingly expensive annual contracts, the appeal of open source software grows. However, if the university needs to allocate resources to developing, maintaining and implementing the software, it is by no means free and this needs to be balanced against the cost of buying an off-the-shelf application. A study of primary and secondary schools in the UK (Becta 2005) showed cost savings for those using open source software, not just in terms of the actual software, which would be expected, but more significantly for the acceptance of open source, in terms of support also. Similarly Skidmore (2005) found that a reduction in costs was one of the major motivations for organizations to switch from proprietary to open source software. However, there can be considerable initial costs involved in transfer, as it often involves developing (or hiring) new skills, transforming materials, and integrating new systems, even if there are savings in the longer term (Drozdik *et al.* 2005).

- *Technical* – there have been a number of technical developments which make the concept of sharing applications or services more viable. Web services is probably the most important of these as it defines a set of standards for sharing services via the internet. The development of web technologies such as XML, J2EE and .Net are also based around open standards and facilitate the development of open source applications.
- *Awareness* – the open source movement has grown in recognition, so it is no longer seen as purely a hobbyist interest. It has gained recognition in two important areas: amongst the IT technicians and support staff in universities and amongst senior managers who are interested in its model. Thus the notion of proposing an open source solution to a particular problem is considered seriously.
- *Interoperability* – there has been a general move towards interoperability within the higher education sector. As we saw in an earlier chapter, this was initially driven by the desire to share content but it became apparent that meaningful education content does not exist in a vacuum and often requires a software application or service. Consequently methods of specifying these in a generic manner are also being developed. This is the basis of the Open Knowledge Initiative (OKI) work at MIT, which is now being taken up by Sakai (see opposite). While interoperability does not itself necessitate an open source approach, it does generate interest in sharing resources, be they content or applications.

It is the convergence of these four factors that has led to the creation of a number of large-scale open source projects in higher education. It seems to be an idea 'whose time has come'. A lot of this activity is centred in the US, but interest is growing globally. In the UK, the Open Source Software Watch conducted a survey of HE and FE institutions in 2003 regarding their attitude and use of OS software (Tanenbaum 2003). They found that 73 per cent of HE respondents reported that their organization had either looked seriously into OS software and/or had already made some decisions on its deployment and that the main reason for deployment was financial.

Many of the recent projects, such as uPortal, Sakai, Shibboleth, are well organized consortia, based around an identified need, and crucially the partners have committed significant resource to them. In this manner they seek to avoid the problem of a community failing to form around the project. While this may help ensure the delivery of a product, it does require significant financial backing, thus reducing one of the initial motivations for adopting OS (although arguably once the software is developed and there is no annual licence fee, it may be cost effective in the long-term).

These projects are all based around interoperability. This is not necessarily the case with all open source; for instance you could create a stand-alone game to teach algebra, say, which made no claim to interoperability, it was simply a useful tool (this is the type of OS application often seen in the K-12 sector). This type of application is useful and is likely to increase as the concept of reuse and resource-sharing becomes more widely accepted. For many such small-scale applications it is debatable whether they represent content or an application, or whether that distinction matters. However, it is the issue of interoperability that is the main focus of attention for large-scale projects. As such, they have openness built into them, so that they can communicate with any other system, as long as it complies with the same open standards.

Open source VLEs

There are a number of open source VLEs and related projects, some of which seek to promote a particular pedagogy, for example Claroline (http://www.claroline.net/), others to provide an open source alternative to commercial VLEs, for eample Bodington (http://bodington.org/index.php), and yet others to devise a service oriented architecture, for example Sakai (http://www.sakaiproject.org/). In this section we will look at three of these, namely Sakai, LAMS and Moodle.

Sakai

The Sakai project was initially founded as a consortium comprising the University of Michigan, Indiana University, MIT, Stanford as well as the Open Knowledge Initiative and the uPortal consortium (who have developed the open source portal, http://www.uportal.org/). There are two overall aims to the project – to develop an architecture that allows a service oriented approach to VLE development and to develop open source tools that would act as components in the architecture. The project thus aims to be both immediately practical and also far-reaching.

The principles of the architecture are described thus (Counterman *et al.* 2004: 2):

- Create a system in which different kinds of applications, some potentially outside of the Sakai environment, can be aggregated to create a single user experience.
- Provide for separation of application and presentation logic.
- Provide an environment that allows tools and services to be migrated and re-used between other Sakai environments, and potentially other (non-Sakai) environments.

- Capture educational, application, common and system capabilities into re-usable services that can be migrated in Sakai and non-Sakai environments.
- Create an environment that allows tools and services to be adapted to local system requirements including enterprise and back office services.

This is indeed a bold set of aims, and ones that if realized would have major implications for VLEs. The members of the consortium deliberately set out to use existing tools for their initial work, for example taking the Samigo assessment tool from Stanford and the workflow tool from Indiana and integrating these with Michigan's collaborative CHEF environment combined with the uPortal specification. This allowed them to meet their goal of releasing some practical software, but they also sought to maintain the goal of making the approach more generalizable. In order to deliver on these goals in a short timespan the project was initially limited to the organizations mentioned above, but has since been opened out. Since their inception in 2003 they have signed up an impressive list of partners, and have also managed to achieve a version 2.0 release that is in operation at the consortium institutions and elsewhere.

In their more practical goal then they have been reasonably successful, in that they have effectively created an open source VLE. It is, perhaps not surprisingly, in the more ambitious goal of creating a service oriented architecture where the jury is still out on Sakai. It may be simply a matter of allowing sufficient time and partners who will create tools that conform to the Sakai approach. Until this has been tested in practice it is difficult to establish the success of the project.

Even without a fully realized service oriented solution (I suspect the 'potentially' in the principles above may turn out to be significant), what the Sakai project has demonstrated is that it is feasible to take components from different providers and integrate these into a reasonably cohesive whole, without creating a system from scratch. As tools and techniques for this progress, and more software is created with this type of integration in mind, then this model of development is likely to be more popular.

Moodle

Moodle is an open source VLE, started and led by Martin Dougiamas. Unlike many VLEs it does not claim to be pedagogically neutral but rather supports a social constructivist approach, by promoting discussion and collaboration. On first encountering Moodle, it isn't dramatically different from many commercial VLEs, and so it is not immediately obvious how it supports the social constructivism approach. It has a similar set of tools, including discussion boards, quizzes, content upload, and assignment handling. Cole contends that the social constructivism is evident in the interface design (CMS here stands for course management systems, synonymous with VLE):

> While tool-centric CMS systems give you a list of tools as the interface, Moodle builds the tools into an interface that makes the learning task central. You can organize your Moodle course by week, by topic, or by a social arrangement.
>
> (Cole 2005: 5)

This is quite a subtle difference, particularly when it is compared with the differences found in some other pedagogically focused VLEs such as LAMS and Colloquia, which immediately feel very different from conventional VLEs. Many commercial, 'tool-centric' VLEs would argue that they allow a similar learning task focus. Cole claims that there are three factors that make Moodle a favourable choice: constructivism, its open source base and the Moodle community. I would argue that it is the last two that have the greatest influence, and Moodle's strength is not that it is particularly different from current VLEs, but rather that it offers a free alternative, that can be extended and adapted. There is an active community of Moodle developers and users, which demonstrates all the benefits of the open source approach. The community (http://www.moodle.org) is an excellent source of advice, development and testing. If someone wants to develop a new feature it is likely that they will find someone to collaborate with here, or at least those who will test it, thus extending the pool of expertise any one individual has access to.

The Moodle open source model is akin to that of Linux, with Dougiamas and his team acting as the gateway to the core code, so they decide which features will be incorporated in the official code base. This prevents code branching, and thus the confusion of multiple alternative versions of the software. However, within any one installation you are free to adapt the code to meet your needs as required.

LAMS

The Learning Activity Management System (LAMS) (http://www.lamsfoundation.org/) is developed by James Dalziel and his team at Macquarie University. The idea behind LAMS is that it promotes an activity based approach to learning. It does this by creating a number of prespecified activities from which an educator can construct a sequence. For example, an educator may arrange a reading task, then set a question for students to vote on, and end with a discussion. The configuration of these tasks can be made quite complex, so for example a number of tasks can be grouped together and given optionality, so students can select one from a range of tasks, or conditions can be set before students can progress, for example a score in an assessment or being released by the educator, and so on.

The activity based approach, rather than the content focused one of many VLEs and standards, is reminiscent of the Learning Design philosophy we saw previously. LAMS is described as being 'Learning Design inspired' (for example Kraan 2003b), which means that it follows the general approach but is not restricted to conforming to the standard. This resolutely pragmatic approach has been quite liberating for the LAMS software, which has managed to reach a level of sophistication that the more pure Learning Design tools have not attained as yet.

Another example of this pragmatic approach is that they initially eschewed a service oriented approach, instead developing tools specifically for LAMS, for example the discussion board was developed for LAMS, and integrated into it. For those with an interest in the service oriented approach, the motivation for doing so lends a cautionary tale – they found that it was quicker to write the tool from scratch than to create a generic interface. This is because of the nature of the integration that a Learning Design approach requires. Dalziel (2005) suggests that in order to create tools that are meaningful from a Learning Design perspective – 'Learning Design aware' tools as he terms them – it was more practical to work this way. Dalziel makes the distinction between 'rich' and 'minimal' component integration, arguing that for the necessary control and flow through a Learning Design driven environment, rich integration is the better option:

> Richly integrated components, as demonstrated in LAMS, are technically more challenging to achieve initially, but provides a seamless, integrated environment for both teachers and learners, with better potential for reliable quality of service.

However, now that the system is stable and robust, the LAMS team is developing a method for describing services so that they can be integrated with LAMS. This will make LAMS more capable of hooking in to existing systems, including VLEs. In order to do this they are creating a LAMS Tool Contract which is defined as 'a set of expected behaviours, registered URLs and API calls that a LAMS Tool has to implement to *talk* to LAMS Core' (Braganza 2006).

Dalziel is often cautious of describing LAMS as a VLE, instead focusing on integrating LAMS into existing VLEs such as Moodle and Blackboard. Part of the reason for this is its suitability to meet all the communication needs in education. LAMS is ideal for event driven communication, for example a discussion as part of a single activity sequence. It is not designed for the more persistent communication that forms an equal part of the educational experience, for example a discussion board that lasts for the duration of a course and is used for general discussion, or a more socially oriented space. However, the State University of New York (SUNY) has decided to adopt LAMS as its main VLE, and use a portal (based on the uPortal technology) for this more persistent type of communication, so it may be that LAMS is beginning to occupy a more central role in the overall MLE configuration.

One of the impressive aspects of LAMS is the ease with which educators and students use it. Because it is based on a simple drag and drop interface and the tools match the types of activities that educators typically want to employ, they very quickly find themselves constructing learning pathways. One of the criticisms of Learning Design is that it is complex and requires a level of expertise to use, although new tools are seeking to address this. There is a LAMS community (http://lamscommunity.org/) where a range of users including those in K12, higher education and training discuss issues and, most significantly, exchange learning sequences. Users will take someone else's pathway, and adapt it to their own needs, typically replacing some resources and modifying some tasks. This community is still in its early days, but it represents the type of reuse that has been promoted by various bodies and experts, but rarely achieved.

In a later chapter we will look at the notion of affordances and seek to examine the extent to which technology encourages particular behaviour. In the case of LAMS it could be argued that not only is it easy to use, but that it actually encourages educators to create e-learning material that is more activity based and thus, many would argue, better suited to the e-learning context.

Open source as a reasonable compromise

There seems to be a good case for the open source approach in the development of educational software. First, there is a natural affinity between the open source and academic communities. The process of contributing code has been compared with that of academic review process. Bergquist and Ljungberg suggest that

> you give away your knowledge, not because you are altruistic, but because that is the way of career progression within the academic field. You give away knowledge and information in return for status and reputation. The acceptance of a gift by a community implies recognition of the status of the donor and the existence of certain reciprocal rights. Scientific contributions are gifts, as authors normally do not receive royalties or other payments for the publication of results in a journal. . . . The open source communities are driven by similar norms. You write a piece of software and provide it to the community. Your contribution is peer reviewed by the owners of a software development project and, if it is good enough, you get your credits in the open source gift economy. A good idea is usable in further research but also gives the owner credits.
>
> (Bergquist and Ljungberg 2001: 318)

Second, many open source contributors are employed in education and many projects start as educational projects, for example Moodle began life as part of Martin Dougiamas' Ph.D. Thus it would make sense that in the area of VLEs, which are so central to the education process in the twenty-first century, that a successful open source solution could be found. It has only been very recently though that open source VLEs have been able to compete with commercial ones in terms of usability and reliability.

If we return to the notion of revolutionaries and democrats that was raised in Chapter 2, then we can think about open source solutions in relation to these two audiences. I argued that a VLE was one of the few systems where these two groups were forced to co-exist, and in an area (teaching and learning) that is so central to their sense of identity. Imagine if researchers in all fields were required to use the same software, and one gets a feeling for the diversity that a VLE needs to accommodate.

With the development of more robust and user-friendly open source solutions, open source VLEs have moved some way towards becoming a mainstream technology. At the same time, because they are open to development and modification, they still satisfy some of the requirements of the revolutionaries. Thus it could be argued that while a commercial VLE is never likely to satisfy the needs of the revolutionaries, an open source one might meet the needs of the democrats. If we return to our normal distribution curve, then the open source VLE potentially covers more of the curve (see Figure 9.1). This is only a recent development, in 2004 say, then the specialist knowledge required to run and use an open source VLE would have placed it more in the revolutionary camp, see Figure 9.2.

Commercial VLEs are probably still superior at meeting the needs of a larger proportion of the democrats, including those towards the tail end (see Figure 9.3). The VLE market is finely balanced at the moment, and the type of institution and audience you are dealing with will influence the decision greatly. It may well be influenced by which of the three groups (revolutionaries, democrats or Luddites) has the loudest voice, which is why a process such as that set out in Chapter 5 is important in eliciting feedback from all groups.

Service oriented architectures

The concept of openness is central to the open source projects we have looked at here. This openness is best personified by the service oriented approach when thinking about VLEs. Even if a system does not fully adhere to it, for example in the case of Moodle, it is still an open system, with described methods for integration. The standards we looked at in the previous two chapters are also a key feature in maintaining and promoting this openness.

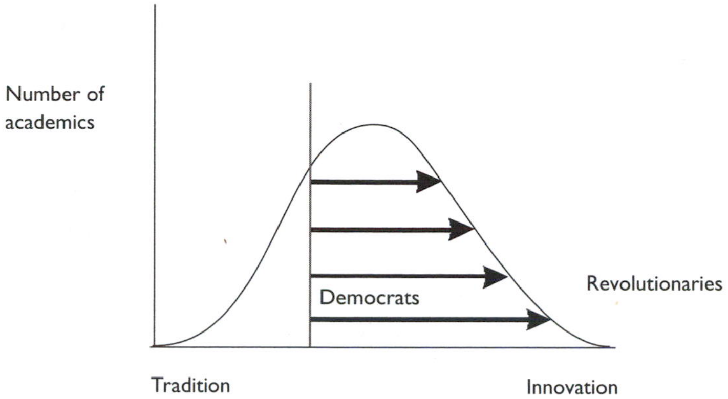

Figure 9.1 Current coverage of open source VLEs.

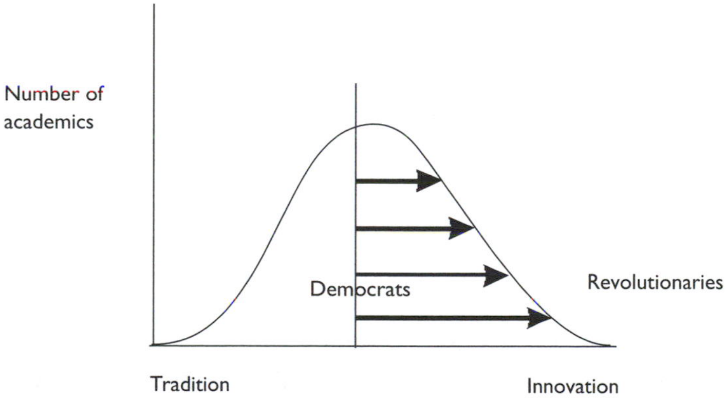

Figure 9.2 Previous coverage of open source VLEs.

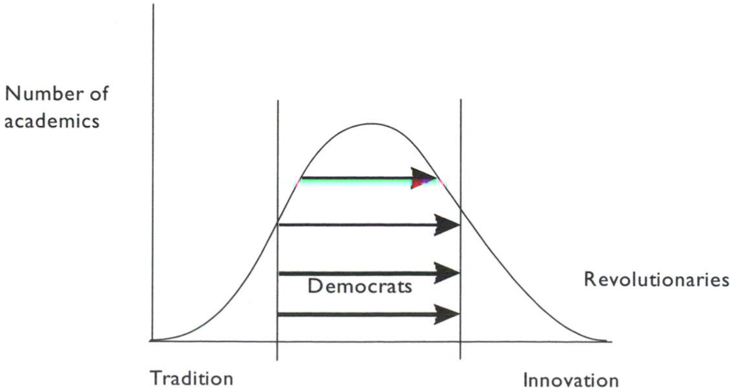

Figure 9.3 Current coverage of commercial VLEs.

The service oriented architecture is based around the central idea that individual tools can be swapped in and out, creating a component based system. In order to realize this three factors need to be in place:

1 Generic descriptions of services that a system can interpret. For example, all bulletin boards perform the same sorts of functions.
2 A methodology for describing these services so that new ones can be added. Any new tools or services that are developed need a means of making themselves open.
3 Tools, services and environments that are amenable to such an approach. This will include being able to expose the main functions of a tool, for example through web services.

Sakai has developed a Tools Portability Profile which seeks to address the first two of these. This is similar in aim to the LAMS Tools Contract, and both of these are not dissimilar to the IMS Tools Interoperability Guidelines, which 'addresses the growing demand for a reusable mechanism for integrating third-party tools with core LMS platforms' (IMS 2006b). The proliferation of these approaches is typical of a movement in its youth, and in the next few years we can expect to see either a consolidation of these or one of them to win out over the others.

Although it has a theoretical and architectural appeal, the service oriented approach is largely untested. The Tasmanian LEAP project is a rare example (LeAP 2004) which uses a service oriented approach to create a flexible VLE:

> The project has guiding principles of interoperability and the use of standards for data and infrastructure. The preferred application architecture model uses a 'service based infrastructure' approach. The reality is that the diversity of products within the educational computing environment makes it impossible to adopt a single approach to application architecture. LeAP considers it good practice to use existing services and create new services as application development progresses.

Until we have many more such systems we cannot evaluate the service oriented approach in general, and particularly some of the potential problems it entails. The three key issues facing the service oriented architecture approach are:

1 Efficiency – by creating sockets and brokering devices, you are increasing the number of steps through which data needs to pass in order to achieve a task. This may not be noticeable at relatively small scale usage, but with large numbers of simultaneous users this increased data handling load could become significant.

2 Richness – by creating generic service descriptions for applications, you are going to miss some of the functions in any one system. To take a small example, in discussion forums some tools have the ability to see the history of a message, i.e. who has read it, when it was posted, and so on. This is a reasonably common but not ubiquitous function, and so the problem facing those who create generic service descriptions is do they include it or not? It may be safer to include such functions, but then any Learning Design, say, that assumes they are present will not work with a system that does not have them. The trade-off between generic descriptions that work across the majority of systems, and rich, application specific descriptions has yet to be worked through.
3 Effort – creating common descriptions is a difficult and time-consuming task, as it involves describing the main functions of all major systems, and then getting agreement from the community, as well as ensuring that technically the systems work together. As the LAMS team found, this work can be a serious hindrance to actually getting something that works, and so the question that the service oriented approach needs to address is whether this is ultimately a worthwhile goal given the amount of effort it takes to attain it.

Conclusion

In this chapter we have looked at a tension that has been present throughout this book in various guises, namely that between open source and proprietary approaches to VLEs. The tension reflects not only a technical approach to the development of software, but also an ideological one, and in the case of VLEs, arguably a pedagogic one also.

There seems to be an affinity between many of the values of the open source community and those in higher education. In addition, open source VLEs may be better suited at meeting the needs of both the revolutionaries and democrats. This may appear to be an exhortation to adopt an open source solution, but that is not my intention. Commercial VLEs play a significant role in the democratization of e-learning, just as commercial operating systems do with computer use in general. Despite much of the evidence and claims that the open source option results in cost savings, for many institutions a commercial VLE represents not only the most convenient solution, but also the most cost effective one. There are a number of hidden costs associated with open source VLEs, not least of which is that they still require a level of expertise to deploy. Although it is possible to simply use an open source VLE without becoming part of the developer community, as happens with systems such as Linux, the current position seems to be that institutions who deploy open source VLEs usually have some active developers also. This is part of the appeal of the open source solution in fact – simply installing a commercial system does not excite many technical staff, but being involved in the deployment of an open source system and being part of a community gives a greater sense of ownership. Thus the open source option often requires a degree of in-house expertise and enthusiasm. The commercial solution can be seen as effectively outsourcing these concerns. However, over recent years open source VLEs have become increasingly part of the mainstream provision, so it is debatable whether this distinction between the two will persist.

Ahmed (2005) suggests that there are four main factors that determine whether an organization will adopt an open source solution:

1. Savings expected from operating an open source system.
2. The need to modify the system's source code.
3. Frustration with delays when fixing bugs and adding functionality to the proprietary system.
4. The influence of champions of open source within the institutions and strength of their relationships to open source communities.

If we ignore the financial consideration for now, then the other factors are interrelated. It is likely that the desire to modify the system's source code will arise from the delays and inability to do so with proprietary software. This arises from the pedagogic needs of different subject areas, and is indicative of a substantial number of revolutionaries within an organization. Similarly, the influence of open source champions demonstrates how key people can sway decisions in a large organization. Advocates of open source are often more devoted, evangelical even, about their favourite software than their proprietary counterparts, partly because the open source model operates on a level of enthusiasm and devotion.

Ahmed goes on to propose six factors that influence the success of an open source migration project:

1. Support from senior management.
2. Commitment from faculty staff to use the system.
3. Support staff with credibility with developers of the open source software.
4. Project team members with open source migration experience.
5. Complexity of migrating content.
6. Complexity of developing new functions, standards and interfaces to the open source system.

The third and fourth factors are significant here (the others could equally apply to any system be it commercial or open source), and suggest that a level of expertise is often required for successful open source deployment.

Having looked at the current state of technology in this chapter, and Chapters 3 and 4, in the next chapter we will consider a possible future direction for VLEs, namely towards a more personalized learning environment.

Chapter 10

Personalization and VLEs

Personalization is often portrayed as the next big thing in e-learning. It has a number of attractions, and plays to the strengths of e-learning. Although a one-on-one tutor is perhaps the most personalized situation you can achieve, it is not very scaleable. Through automation e-learning has the potential to offer personalization on a large scale.

So, what do people mean when they talk about personalization in education? The first point to appreciate is that personalization is often a shorthand for saying 'customization and personalization', where customization is changes made by the user to their learning environment or content, and personalization is changes or choices made by the system. Thus a user may choose to have news feeds from the BBC into their portal, which is customization, and at the same time automatically receive a feed from the American Psychological Association because they are studying psychology, which is an example of personalization. Who actually makes the choice is only one element in the process, however, and the overall framework that needs to be in place is the same for both customization and personalization, hence they are bundled together.

With regards to VLEs, there are two flavours of personalization. The first is personalization of content and information, and the second is personalization of tools and services. The second of these has led to the concept of a personal learning environment (PLE).

Personalized content

The acquisition of data about a user allows a system to adapt the content it offers, so there is a move away from a homogenous approach to content, to a more tailored, personalized set of learning materials. The most common form of personalization encountered online is through e-commerce sites such as Amazon. Here the site combines two powerful data techniques, namely monitoring of previous behaviour and data mining. Monitoring is fairly straightforward, as the system will record the items you have purchased, browsed, added to a wishlist and so forth. Data mining involves looking at the behaviour of large groups of users and uncovering patterns of behaviour. In the case of Amazon this leads to the recommendations you receive, for example 'Customers who bought this book also bought. . . .'

In terms of e-learning, monitoring can be combined with diagnostic tests, for example to determine preferred learning styles. A student can then be offered material that reflects this preferred style (for example learners with a preference for visual material may receive more diagrams or animations), and also seeks to address areas where students have shown either an ability to go beyond the current material or a need for remedial content, based on their performances in assessment. By setting preferences users can also structure the display, for example choosing between navigation methods.

The ultimate aim of personalization is to offer material that meets the needs of the individual learner at the exact moment they need that information. This is particularly true in corporate settings, where just-in-time learning is seen as both more effective and cost-efficient. For example Adler and Rae (2002) talk of a personalized e-learning future:

> Imagine that in the future you will have your own personalized learning environment that reflects your individual style and learning needs, and is instantly available. Not only will it be your one point of learning entry for everything you need to learn, but it will continue to learn as you learn and modify its behavior based on interacting with you over time.

Data mining can aid the process by identifying patterns of behaviour. This can be at the recommendations type level – suggesting or providing similar resources based on correlations. It could also be used to uncover certain student behaviours, for example those who are about to drop out of a course tend to exhibit certain patterns of behaviour, and so intervention may be possible.

The other major area of interest in personalization is that of accessibility. If there is a sufficient range of resources available, and these are suitably described, then it is possible to automatically provide alternatives that suit the specific needs of any user, provided there is data on the user. For example students with visual impairment may prefer a text-only version of a resource so it is more easily read by text readers. There is some debate though as to the extent to which the system rather than the user should make these choices, and also whether it encourages a dual stream approach, with disabled users not receiving the same resources as others.

To call this personalization of content is perhaps a bit misleading. It is not that the material is adapted specifically for the user, in the same way that a human educator would adjust what they are saying to suit the needs of an individual student. There is some work in this area, based on artificial intelligence techniques using intelligent agents, but that is not what is usually meant by personalization in e-learning. Rather it is the provision of more suitable content from a large pool of resources. In order for this to be realized there are four factors that need to be in place:

- Content needs to be suitably chunked – large pieces of content, for example books, are unlikely to provide sufficient variation to meet the needs of personalization. Smaller chunks, such as learning objects, are more suitable if you wish to realize a highly adaptable and reconfigurable set of resources.
- Content is suitably described – it's unavoidably metadata again. If resources are to be used to match against learning styles, for instance, then there needs to be an associated field (or fields) in the metadata that can be used. This can either be a direct mapping, in which case a 'Learning Style' field needs to be completed, or a proxy, for example files containing images might be deemed more suitable for learners with a visual preference.
- Sufficient range of content – in order for personalization to work and to be worthwhile, then there needs to be a wide range of resources to draw upon which will meet the different needs and preferences of users.
- Rich user data – if content is suitably described then the other side of the equation that needs to be present for personalization is data about the user. In this respect education has an advantage over e-commerce sites, since users interact with the material to a far greater extent. VLEs therefore have the data gathered from quizzes and tests which have an element of compulsion to them that is not present in e-commerce. For VLEs there is also the full range of other tools, each of which can provide a rich set of data, for example the number and frequency of posts in a discussion forum, the time spent looking at pages, the resources accessed and so on. Combined with this is the data gathered from related systems we saw in Chapter 6, most notably the student record system, but others such as the library will also have relevant information.

This is not an inconsiderable set of requirements, and so it is no surprise that personalization is something talked about but rarely seen in e-learning, beyond the most basic level. None of these requirements necessitate a substantial improvement or change in VLE technology, however. Rather what is required are changes to practice, for example in producing sufficient learning object type content, and a collective will to create such a system, for example by focusing on the development of pools of content rather than specific courses. While personalized content is a version of personalization that can occur with existing systems, personal learning environments require a much more significant rethinking of current technology, and we will look at these next.

Personal learning environments

The idea behind a PLE is that users amass or create a collection of tools for themselves, which constitute their own learning environment. Thus a user may have an instant messaging client, a blog, a note-taking tool, an e-portfolio and so on, which are different from anyone else's. The PLE provides a way of linking these together for the user and then integrating them with institutional systems. Work on PLEs is still at a very early stage, but their possible advantages include:

- They better meet the needs of the lifelong learner who interacts with a succession of institutions, each of which has their own VLE.
- The individual is the owner of content and information, not the institution.
- The user has a collection of tools that suit their needs and preferences.
- They offer choice and diversity as to how tasks are realized, rather than being specified by the educator.
- They promote a degree of user responsibility and ownership.
- New tools and software can be integrated easily by any single user, rather than necessitating an enterprise-wide integration.

A PLE embodies a very learner-centric view of how technologies should be configured, and thus it is closely allied with a constructivist type approach to learning. There is also a link with the service oriented approaches we have seen. If you view VLEs as a set of services aggregated together, then these can be disaggregated easily and new components slotted in, but this time by the user and not the institution.

Green *et al.* (2004) argue that

> The logic of education systems should be reversed so that it is the system that conforms to the learner, rather than the learner to the system. This is the essence of personalization. It demands a system capable of offering bespoke support for each individual that recognizes and builds upon their diverse strengths, interests, abilities and needs in order to foster engaged and independent learners able to reach their full potential.

It is difficult to argue with the sentiment behind this statement, but it carries several implications, which need to be addressed if PLEs are to become anything more than an interesting research project. There are some considerable cultural and technological barriers they would need to overcome:

1 Support – the support issues for an institution and educators would be extremely complex if each user had a different set of tools, and so would most likely be passed on to the individual. One of the reasons why current VLEs have been successful is that they allow universities to centralize

support and thus ensure a certain level of competence and quality of experience.

2 Quality assurance – increasingly universities need to ensure a certain quality of provision. This would be difficult to maintain and predict if everyone is using different tools.
3 Suitability – while the learner-centric notion has much about it which is admirable, we should also be aware that sometimes the student is not the best judge of what is the best approach. In this context this could mean they continue to use a tool when a different one is better suited to the purpose, or they are not exposed to new technologies.
4 Negotiation of activity – although the choice and flexibility in this approach is a strength, it could also create a significant overhead in negotiation. For example group activities would be difficult to achieve if everyone used their own tools. While there may be some standardization and compatibility between systems (for example different IM clients may be able to communicate), this is difficult to envisage between different categories of systems (for example IM and asynchronous tools). Therefore there would need to be negotiation between students as to which tools to use.
5 Technological complexity – although the service oriented approaches and standardization will help, it would still be an enormously complex task to enable the range of different tools to integrate with those systems required by an institution and even more problematic if one has to assume a novice user.

In fashion it is often suggested that if you stay still long enough, trends will come back around to where you are, but with some modification. This is true with educational trends also, as any teacher who has lived through successive government initiatives can tell you. In terms of e-learning technologies, the initial trend was for proprietary software clients that were installed on everyone's computer. So you would have separate pieces of software for email, discussion forums, online simulations, etc. Then the web came along and the web browser became the ubiquitous interface. This was a significant step forward and was partly responsible for the phenomenal growth of internet usage in the nineties. Now you could use any browser to access most of the functions you wanted to perform online. This is very useful if you log in from different locations, as you don't need to rely on multiple versions of different software clients being available. It also means you can integrate different tools as they are operating within the same browser framework, for example you can link discussion forums and content easily, without the need for users to start up different pieces of software. However, there is often a loss of richness and speed in using a web version of a system compared to the dedicated software client.

With PLEs the fashion seems to have come full circle again, and the talk is now of rich, desktop clients once again. Two reasons are put forward as the main advantages of this approach, one of which I feel is valid, and the other less so. The first, more powerful argument, is the ability for the user to create a rich environment with complex functionality, which would be difficult to achieve through a web browser. The software is housed on the user's machine, and not located remotely on a server, which means that the transactions are quicker and the level of control greater. The second argument put forward is that a client allows the user to work offline, since the connection with the server is not required. While this is important for users sometimes, it is something of a red herring. Most users can easily arrange tasks for periods when they know they will be offline, for example downloading documents for reading. It runs counter to the trend in society for almost ubiquitous connectivity. There *may* be times when you want to take your mobile device to the top of a mountain to study, but these are not so frequent as to necessitate the massive development and cultural effort that a PLE-oriented system requires.

PLEs sit very firmly in the revolutionaries camp, and much of the rhetoric that surrounds them portrays current VLEs as an educational menace, for instance in his blog Derek Morrisson (2005) suggests that 'I kind of feel our current VLEs . . . urgently need to be replaced with a better design and, who knows, PLEs may go some way towards this day'. As with many trends that come from deep within the revolutionaries' camp, there is something at the core of these claims that will work its way into the mainstream, although not in quite the way that the revolutionaries might envisage. What the PLE work reveals and acknowledges is the growing use of technologies by learners. VLEs are often operating on an assumption of zero experience and competence (which is the safest thing to do, and for some students, valid). Higher education has not really begun to address the implications of 'digital natives' as Prensky (2001) terms them, coming into the higher education context with familiarity and loyalty to a number of different technologies.

The tension here is between institutional and individual technologies. VLEs are an institutional response to the opportunities of the internet. Most of the tools we looked at in Chapter 4 such as blogs and instant messaging are based around the individual. An e-portfolio is a good example of this tension. Many universities are beginning to develop or buy institutional e-portfolio systems, so that they provide all students with this tool and use it in specific courses and for institutional aims, for example as a means of assessment. However, the e-portfolio is an individual tool and one of the main drivers behind them is their ability to collate information and learning across institutions. So, should an e-portfolio be a tool that a user brings to an institution or one that an institution provides for everyone? Our old friend interoperability goes some way to solving the dilemma, since it means data can be ported between applications, but it is unlikely to be the complete solution, and many of the problems with the PLE outlined above, such as support and guaranteed level of provision, will remain.

Some of the implicit and explicit criticism of current VLEs that is found in the PLE work is valid, but this does not necessarily mean that the PLE is the solution. Some of the complaints, for example the 'one size does not fit all' claim, could be addressed by making VLEs better, either in terms of pedagogy or customization. One could envisage a rich set of tools being offered to students via VLEs, with customizable and personalized feeds, interfaces and tool selection, which would go some way to achieving the aims set out for PLEs.

The desirability of personalization

The implicit assumption underlying many of the visions of a more personalized e-learning future is that personalization is always desirable, that it is an end point we all want to achieve. While there are many benefits of a more personalized approach, and it is one of the advantages that e-learning can offer over the mass provision of lectures, it is worth addressing the downside of personalization. I would suggest that there are four issues surrounding personalization which are often ignored by its proponents:

1. Commonality of experience – at one extreme of personalization the course as we currently conceive of it is replaced by a course for every learner. There is no single course, but rather highly individualized collections of resources based on each learner's needs and preferences. What is lost in such a highly learner-centric future is the shared experience of studying the same course. It becomes difficult to discuss tasks or content if everyone is studying a different set of material. As well as being limiting pedagogically (it would make collaborative activities difficult to realize for instance), it also undervalues the social dimension that is part of the appeal of higher education. This may be less pertinent with corporate training and staff development, and so this may be where personalized learning finds its truest expression.
2. Exposure to different approaches – if resources are selected according to a user's preferred learning style, there is a danger that they are not exposed to different approaches. Part of the role of higher education is to broaden the range of learning experiences a student has, and not just the content they study. For example many students might prefer to avoid group work, but it is commonly accepted that being able to work as part of a team is a key characteristic of graduates in general and a trait employers will require. If a personalized approach allowed users to avoid this type of approach then it would ultimately be providing a disservice to students. Much of the personalization rhetoric is bound up with the idea of student as customer, where they receive the content they prefer. However, there are still times when it is necessary to consider the student as, well, a student.
3. Privacy – this is a very large and contentious topic and one which is likely to be tested in the courts in coming years. Throughout this chapter

I have made reference to gathering large amounts of user data, with the assumption that it is desirable to do so. This may not be the case, even if that data is being used for the student's benefit (or at least that is the intention). There are several issues here that need to be explored. The first is the effect that gathering such data has on student behaviour. Land and Bayne (2004) argue that monitoring in VLEs is more akin to surveillance. They use the analogy of Jeremy Bentham's Panopticon, a design for prisons, whereby every cell can be seen from a central tower. Foucault (1979) used the panopticon concept to analyze changes in power structures, which moved from being driven primarily by punishment to being controlled by surveillance. This is a very hierarchical model, and at some variance with the more egalitarian, community based approaches espoused by many e-learning advocates. Another potentially damaging by-product of monitoring is that once users know they are being monitored then they are likely to exhibit the behaviour that they think the monitor wants. In an educational context this could be inhibiting for many of the more exploratory pedagogic approaches. This is true even if they are not being continually monitored. There is also the issue of security, and access to data, which becomes increasingly difficult to manage when we have the sort of distributed system outlined in a service oriented architecture, where data is used by many different systems. The most significant factor is the degree to which e-learning will demand the surrender of privacy, because so many systems require it to work successfully. Many of the technologies we looked at in Chapter 4 are social, community based ones, which require a degree of personal information and privacy to be surrendered. If this becomes the norm, then any student who wishes to maintain a high degree of privacy (and there may be very serious reasons for doing so, such as escaping persecution) could find themselves unable to partake in the full range of learning experiences on a personalized course.

4 Content focus – although it is not necessarily the case, much of the discussion in personalization tends to focus around content. There is a danger that this is at the expense of the more social, dialogic components, and the provision of adaptive content is seen as the ultimate goal in e-learning. As I have already mentioned, the realization of a personalized learning system may preclude or inhibit the communication aspect of learning because the commonality of experience is reduced and the logistics of arranging a collaborative task between users who are essentially studying different courses becomes too complex. In Chapter 1 I argued that the successful combination of the internet's potential as both a content and communication medium was the key to success in e-learning. If personalization skews the balance in favour of content then the benefits it provides may be something of a Pyrrhic victory.

To these we could also add the more basic issue of cost effectiveness. A 2003 report (Jupiter Research 2003) looked at personalization in commercial sites and found that such sites were four times more expensive to run than standard sites, and provided few positive benefits. These costs have probably been reduced since this time, with the improvement of database technologies designed to offer personalization services, but the point remains that without a clear rationale and direction for personalization, it will be a costly exercise with no clear gain.

Conclusion

In this chapter we have looked at the trend towards personalization in VLEs. This can be seen as the provision of suitable content, which matches the needs of a particular user. There is also growing interest in the creation of PLEs, which are based around a personal collection of tools for each user.

While personalization is generally promoted as desirable from the learner's perspective, there are a number of issues surrounding personalization that need to be addressed, including the impact it would have upon the social dimension of study and the privacy implications.

The personalized approach to e-learning does represent a fundamental shift in how we think about education. As with e-learning in general, as soon as you begin to unpick the implications it has for education, then it quickly becomes apparent that there are few areas of education that would remain untouched by such a ground shift in practice. Any change in educational practice is most readily reflected in the impact it has on assessment, since this sits at the heart of the formal education system. In a personalized learning future the kind of blanket assessment methods we currently employ, most readily embodied in the conventional exam, become difficult to justify since students will have had different content, based on different starting points. The focus then is more around competencies, and regardless of the actual content you have received, certain competencies should be achieved. Related to this the concept of a course becomes meaningless, and thus all the associated administrative procedures also need modification. Most universities, and VLEs, use the course as their main administrative unit, and so the removal of this has major implications. The role of the academic is also altered in such a scenario, with perhaps more emphasis being placed either on the support of students, or the creation of general content. The support that can be provided also becomes problematic, since it would be increasingly difficult to be aware of all the content students could be studying.

None of these issues are insurmountable, but given the often conservative nature of universities a certain degree of skepticism regarding some of the claims surrounding personalized learning is probably wise. As with most innovations what we are likely to see is some middle ground between the current homogenous approach and the fully personalized version, so for instance VLEs will permit users to integrate their preferred tool within the overall framework, while providing a default option for those who do not have one.

Chapter 11

Affordances and patterns

In this chapter we will consider two conceptual approaches which can be applied to educational technology, namely affordances and patterns. These potentially offer a means of describing technologies and pedagogies in conceptual terms, and facilitating the selection of technology to suit a particular pedagogy and the selection of a pedagogy to suit a desired outcome.

Both approaches are not without their critics, however, and throughout this chapter you should consider whether the approaches actually provide any benefit, or offer any new insights into how we use educational technologies.

Affordances

Much of the discussion around affordances becomes mired in definitions, with corresponding confusion as to what the term actually means (McGrenere and Ho 2000). The reason for this is that it is a term that has come from one domain (perception and ecology) to be used in another (software design), with a subsequent alteration in its meaning. The term was initially proposed by Gibson (1979: 143) to describe what interaction the environment offers an organism. He states that 'the medium, substances, surfaces, objects, places and other animals have affordances for a given animal. They offer benefit or injury, life or death.' For example, for a duck, water affords swimming. The same environment will have different affordances for different organisms. Affordances are a means of describing how the organism perceives its environment, with the emphasis on interaction.

The concept was then popularized by Norman (1988: 9) who applied it to the design of many everyday objects. His classic example is that of a door handle, which affords pulling. He suggested that 'affordances provide strong clues to the operation of things' and poor design can be explained in terms of a lack of affordances. The purpose of features or objects should be signaled by their design, and not require further explanation. Norman's work did much to broaden the use of the term, although it also led to confusion. As Boyle and Cook (2004: 296) note, 'Norman conflates two important but different things – designing the utility of an object and designing the way in which that utility is conveyed to the user. In his later work Norman acknowledges the confusion and seeks to distinguish "*real* from *perceived* affordances"'. Real affordances are those that are constrained by the environment, for example a door that only opens one way so the handle *has* to be pulled. Perceived affordances are ones we attribute to features, and are particularly relevant in software design, for example a scroll bar might have the perceived affordance of scrolling, but only if the cursor were constrained within that space would it be a real affordance. The distinction is probably not significant for our purposes, but it is indicative of the type of debate and confusion surrounding the term.

Affordances were then applied to the design of software, and human–computer interaction (for example Gaver 1991), so for example, a button that seems to protrude affords clicking. The concept was then applied to educational technology (for example Laurillard *et al.* 2000). Kreijns *et al.* (2002) extend the concept to that of social affordances, in the context of 'computer-supported collaborative learning environments' (CSCL). They define social affordances as 'properties of CSCL environment that act as social-contextual facilitators relevant for the learner's social interactions. When they are perceptible, they invite the learner to act in accordance with the perceived affordances, i.e. start a task or non-task related interaction or communication.'

The use of the term now becomes decidedly post-Gibsonian, but it is still focused on the interaction between user and tool. Affordances are being applied to higher cognitive functions, such as communication, rather than the simple interaction with an object such as a handle or button. It is with this extension to more complex actions that it becomes useful in terms of educational technology. Conole and Dyke (2004) suggest a taxonomy of ten affordances for computers in education, for example they argue that 'asynchronous technologies (in particular) offer the potential for encouraging reflection and critique, with users engaging in discussions over a longer time frame than is possible in face-to-face discussions'.

If we consider some of the communication tools commonly found in VLEs and those discussed in Chapter 4, it is possible to create a list of affordances they provide (see Table 11.1). In this case we will consider communication affordances, that is how the technologies influence the types of communication that take place. In terms of education we can define six types of communication:

- Reflective – contains elements that relate to the individual's experience.
- Analytical – analyzes, argues or proposes an idea.
- Social – not specifically focused on the subject area, and may be more chat-like.
- Task – focused on a specific task.
- Communal – either focuses on, or helps to create and maintain, the student community.
- Informal/formal – the communication may be informal or more formal in style.

Table 11.1 Communication affordances for different communication technologies.

Tool	*Communication affordance*
Discussion board	Reflective, analytical, social, task, mid-formality
Audio/video conferencing	Social, task, informal
Shared whiteboard	Task
Blogs	Reflective, informal
Wikis	Communal
Podcasting	Reflective
Social software	Communal
Structured conferencing	Analytical, task, formal
Instant messaging	Social, informal
E-portfolios	Reflective, formal

If we look at Table 11.1 it is evident why asynchronous discussion tools have dominated much of the communication in VLEs. They satisfy most of the communication types to a reasonable degree. However, they do not meet all of them, and for the ones they do meet, they may not be as suitable as other tools. To this end, the suggested affordances may need further division, for example the type of reflection that occurs in an asynchronous discussion board might be different from that which occurs over an extended period in a blog.

There will also be different perspectives one could take on communication, for example one could consider the immediacy of communication, or use a formal categorization of communication, such as Bales' (1950) small group interaction analysis, which divides communication into four categories.

If we accept that affordances exist, it is difficult to say whether they arise because the technology itself influences how the user interacts, or whether the user conforms to the norms of communication as they see them. For example, does using an instant messaging client itself encourage people to use an informal, chatty style of communication or do they communicate in that way because everyone else does? It probably does not matter which way round the influence is, and it may be that both reasons are valid. You can think of affordances as a form of technological compliance; for example, if you put people in a fast car, they tend to drive faster. Is this because the technology suggests, and permits, it, or because they have a socially determined model of how to behave in a fast car? Either way, if you want someone to drive fast then putting them in a Ferrari is a better bet than putting them in a van, even if the van is capable of going fast. The same applies with our communication affordances – if you want students to forge a community then wikis would be useful, and if you want them to engage in quick, social type interaction, then instant messaging is useful.

One of the problems with affordances is that they are based on the individual's experience so, for example, the fast driving affordance assumes that the person can drive. This means that an affordance may not be apparent to some people, depending on their experience and personality. However, one can think of common types of behaviour or communication in certain types of tool, and thus the judicious selection of a tool will generally, but not always, promote that type of communication amongst students. Similarly users may have different affordances than the ones that are assumed or intended. Wijekumar *et al.* (2006) investigated K-12 students' use of ICT and suggest that for many children the computer has a 'game affordance', rather than a learning one. They state that 'one student reported how another computer learning tool was introduced in their school and most students turned the learning environment into a game of trying to give as many incorrect responses as possible to the system'.

Patterns

Like affordances, the concept of patterns is one that has come from another domain, this time architectural design, and then been applied to software. The concept of patterns was initiated by Christopher Alexander and colleagues (Alexander 1979, Alexander *et al.* 1977), who suggested that the reason much modern architecture (in the 1960s) failed people was because it lacked certain qualities. Alexander *et al.* attempted to devise a language and set of tools for aiding the design process in order to capture these qualities. The result was the concept of patterns, which essentially seek to provide a solution to a problem. This is perhaps their most useful contribution, in that they encourage the designer to think in terms of problems and then set about describing means of solving them. Alexander *et al.* (1977) state that a pattern

> describes a problem which occurs over and over again in our environment, and then describes the core of the solution to that problem, in such a way that you can use this solution a million times over, without ever doing it the same way twice.

This approach was then applied to software design (for example Gamma *et al.* 1995), and then more recently to pedagogy. For example the Pedagogical Patterns Project (http://www.pedagogicalpatterns.org/) seeks to describe a set of abstract patterns that can be used to inform teaching. Similarly the E-LEN project (http://www2.tisip.no/E-LEN/) uses patterns to promote reuse of teaching approaches and as a means of offering guidance to those creating e-learning materials. As part of the project Joseph Bergin (2000) provides a number of patterns used in teaching computer science, for example, "Consistent Metaphor", which he describes thus: 'When teaching a complex topic outside a student's normal experience, find a complex and consistent metaphor for the topic being taught. The basis of the metaphor needs to be known to the students.' The pattern is then described using a template derived from Alexander, so there are fields for:

- Problem/issue – describes the problem you are trying to solve.
- Audience/context – describes the context in which the problem arises.
- Forces – outlines the forces at work which create the tension.
- Solution – the suggested solution to the problem.
- Discussion/consequences/implementation – a space that can be used to add more notes that can aid others.
- Special resources – states whether any equipment or resources are required.
- Related patterns – links to any other patterns that may have a bearing.
- Example instances – a place to provide any examples.

Others use a more simple situation–problem–solution template for describing patterns. For example, Pemberton and Griffiths (1998) give this example from interface design:

Show computer is thinking pattern
Situation – operations can take a long time.
Problem – people need to be warned when an operation is going to take a substantial amount of time, otherwise they may assume something has gone wrong. They are unwilling to sit and wait if the wait is to be fruitless, but on the other hand they do not want to confuse the system by reissuing commands unnecessarily.
A solution – give special feedback for lengthy operations. Examples would include changing the cursor to a watch or egg timer, showing a timeline, filling a time-bar and so on.

What patterns provide us with is both a means of conceptualizing a domain, by thinking in terms of abstract problems and solutions, and then a means of describing these through the use of the sort of templates set out above. However, as with any level of abstraction, they are only useful to a certain degree. As Fricke and Voelker (2000) warn, 'there are no "magic techniques". That's why this pattern language does not give recipes that say "Do this, and everything is fine!" It only hints at proven techniques and describes them as a pattern language.'

Patterns are not confined to pedagogy, however, and have been used in software design. They could be seen as an alternative to affordances in describing technology in more generic terms. For example, the following might be a valid pattern for VLEs:

Situation – students should engage in discussion that is closely linked to course content.
Problem – often there is a schism between content and discussion, so that students either do not engage in any discussion or it is not closely linked to the content.

Solution – embed discussion tools within the content, so students do not need to come out of the content or start a new tool, but can engage in discussion when it is relevant.

Examples – the D3E (Digital Document Discourse Environment) tool (http://d3e.sourceforge.net/index.html) allows asynchronous discussion to be embedded within content. Swarming technology such as Eyebees (http://www.eyebees.com) shows which users are looking at particular pages. You can then invite them into a synchronous discussion. Collaborative and virtual meeting tools, such as Webex (http://www.webex.com) and Groove (http://www.groove.net/), allow users to engage in discussion around shared documents.

Affordances, patterns and VLEs

You may be thinking that this is all very interesting, but what has it to do with VLEs? In Chapter 3 I argued that you could accommodate a wide range of pedagogies within current VLEs. While this is true, it is difficult to argue that current VLEs *afford* many of these pedagogies. It requires much intervention and planning to realize many of them. Norman suggested that the use of a tool should be apparent, and to extend this, it is often this apparent use that becomes the main use of a tool, whatever the intended use was. Gall and Breeze (2005: 425) compared the use of music composition software and found that one had better affordances (or interface design), so that students could quickly create compositions without a great deal of specialist knowledge, claiming that 'the transparent interface and the lack of need to develop complex technological skills allowed the pupil to compose quickly before creative ideas were lost.' Consider now an academic coming to a VLE. What are the affordances it offers? For most current VLEs it affords a very content-driven, linear model. This is not surprising as, in order to sell it to universities, the designers have constructed VLEs so that they map onto existing practices rather than necessitating a completely new way of working. It is easy to upload and structure content and thus create a course which is akin to a series of lectures. In Chapter 9 we encountered the LAMS system, and I mentioned that many people find it quite instinctive to use, and are very soon designing activity-based e-learning. Another way of putting it is that LAMS affords an activity-based approach, and arguably this is a better way of realizing e-learning. Similarly, when Cole (2005: 5) argues that most VLEs 'support a content model that encourages instructors to upload a lot of static content, Moodle focuses on tools for discussion and sharing artefacts', he could be suggesting that Moodle has different affordances from conventional VLEs. Thinking in terms of affordances, then, helps educators and designers determine the type of VLE they wish to use and the tools it should contain.

In terms of VLEs the patterns approach potentially offers a means of describing the other side of the e-learning equation, namely that of pedagogy.

If we can describe pedagogies, activity structures or learning outcomes in a canonical fashion, then we can match these against the technical description we have set out in affordances.

What both affordances and patterns provide is a means of thinking and talking about technology and pedagogy in a more abstract manner. This allows us to be one step removed from the particular instance we are involved in, for example a specific course, and thus reason in more general terms about what it is we wish to achieve. Imagine I was designing a course on the modern novel. There are several approaches I could take to course design, for example:

- Learning outcomes or objectives – I could determine the range of knowledge, skills and abilities that students should acquire, and set about devising content and activities to satisfy these.
- Pragmatic – I could find what resources were available (in terms of books, learning objects, software and people) and construct a course around these.
- Curriculum driven – I could examine the other courses available and ensure that this course covered the subjects the others did not, thus making a complete curriculum.
- External accreditation – the influence of external bodies and associated accreditation could be the main influence.
- Pedagogy – a particular pedagogy could underlie the whole course.
- Content – I could draw up a list of subject areas that need to be covered and then set about 'filling' each of these.

In reality most course design is a complex amalgamation of all these various drivers, but some will be more dominant than others. Vocational courses for example are often entirely determined by the external accrediting body, with little room for variation.

If we now look at how an affordance and pattern based approach might be used, we can see how it both fits and contrasts with the existing methods. If my goal is to get students to appreciate the role of style in the novel, then I might look at a set of pedagogical patterns, and find that one entitled 'Stylistic role play' looks useful. The pattern is described thus:

- Problem – students experience a range of different communication styles and do not always appreciate the effect that the nature of the communication plays on their reaction to the message.
- Context – particularly online information comes in many different styles. The tone, style and nature of that communication can be as significant as its content.
- Solution – ask students to role play conveying the same information, but from different perspectives.
- Example – in a residential course on health and safety groups of students are asked to produce presentations that all explain one area (such as

> electricity) in different styles (for example factual, humourous, image intensive, story-based, etc.). They then appraise the presentations on different criteria (for example interest, coverage, etc.). In a slight modification, students role play being at the United Nations and discuss a particular topic in different areas, for example break out rooms, corridors, main hall, etc. They analyze the different types of discussion and information they had in these environments.

I decide that a modification of this pattern would meet my needs, by requiring students to write a short scene in the style of different authors, for example Ernest Hemingway, Vladimir Nabokov, Toni Morrisson. They will then discuss the different effect of the style according to supplied criteria.

Now I need to determine what the best technology would be to achieve this. I look at a list of affordances for the tools we have available and find that a structured conferencing tool has the affordance of 'promoting detailed and reflective discussion, focused on a specific task, with an element of compulsion'. This suits my needs for the initial round, but then I want a more informal discussion, so I opt for a synchronous chat session. I then set up the activity using a structured conferencing system for the first week, and ending with a synchronous chat session at the end.

There are several points to note about this approach. First, that the example patterns are in a very different domain to the one in which it is to be employed. That there is some transfer between these suggests that there is benefit to be gained in thinking about pedagogy in a more generic fashion. Second, the patterns are reasonably neutral regarding their medium, they could be conducted face to face or online, and with a variety of technologies. Lastly, the affordances match my interpretation of this pattern, after I have adapted it to my specific needs.

Conclusions

In this chapter we have looked at two methods of developing canonical descriptions of technologies and teaching that can be adapted for educational technology. By searching for more generic descriptions, the commonality between different subject areas and tools can be seen. The disadvantage is that, as with any abstraction, there comes a point where it becomes so general as to be meaningless. For Goodyear *et al.* (2004) patterns in particular offer a means around this, arguing that

> existing approaches to supporting design are not very satisfactory. In particular, it is hard to strike an appropriate balance between rigour and prescriptiveness and to find appropriate levels of generality. . . . In our view, [Alexander] strikes the right balance between rigour and prescriptiveness – offering useful guidance without constraining creativity and providing helpful foci for design.

This is where the real debate with affordances and patterns lies. As Boyle and Cook rightly ask, 'Does the concept of affordances really help?' To what extent could one talk about simply good interface design for affordances, or learning outcomes for pedagogical patterns without the need to appropriate new terms that carry a baggage of potential confusion to our needs? This gets us to the core of the approach in my view. *If* they provide a way of thinking, and talking, about technology and teaching that offers us something different then, whatever the underlying theory, they are useful concepts.

There is a similarity between patterns, affordances and the Learning Design approach we looked at earlier. All of these seek to provide generic descriptions that are reusable in different contexts. McAndrew *et al.* (2006) suggest that patterns, Learning Design and the LAMS system can all be seen as similar, arguing that 'in each case there is a sense in which their application is neutral and they may be exploited in a variety of ways'. They go on to demonstrate this by describing the same task using each of the three methods.

The extent to which these concepts can, and should, be formalized is debatable. As we saw with some of the educational technology standards, we can be presented with something of a dilemma here. In order to avoid multiple meanings and to move the approach forwards it is necessary to provide a formal description, but in doing so one creates a specification that is complex or restrictive and thus alienates the very people it is intended to help. Through the use of tools such as authoring wizards or LAMS, it is possible that both affordances and patterns can overcome this dilemma.

Patterns also return us to a central theme in this book, namely that of democratization. For Alexander patterns were a method for democratizing architectural design, because they were an approach that could be understood by non-experts. This is the appeal of both affordances and patterns – they offer a means of bridging the gap between e-learning technologies and practitioners. As such they are examples of what Conole (2006) calls 'mediating artefacts', borrowing the term from Vygotsky and Engelstrom, which 'help practitioners and students to make informed decisions and choices in order to undertake specific teaching and learning activities'. Conole argues that mediating artefacts become increasingly important when there is increased complexity and change in the environment, which is certainly the case in e-learning. In the chapter on Learning Design I suggested that one of the benefits of the approach was that it acted as a method for the educator to articulate what they wanted to achieve, and record these design decisions. In this role, Learning Design can be seen as a mediating artefact also, and this is how Laurillard and McAndrew (2003) are viewing it when they suggest that Learning Design can become the catalyst in the creation of a more open approach to supporting the community of learning technologists and academic teachers. Other examples of mediating artefacts might include case studies, UML and examples of best practice.

Chapter 12

Case studies

In this chapter we will return to some of the themes that have arisen in the book, particularly the deployment of VLEs within an organization, the choice of VLEs, the open source and proprietary debate and the relationship of the VLE with other systems. This will be realized by looking at four case studies in the selection of VLEs. The four cases studies are the UK Open University, The State University of New York, Deakin University and the New Zealand Open Source VLE project.

The Open University

The UK Open University (UKOU) is a purely distance education university, and often operates with large student numbers, for instance there are around 250,000 registered users on its discussion systems and some courses have cohorts in excess of 10,000. As such, the twin demands of distance and scale mean that the requirements it has of educational technologies are not always the same as those of more traditional, campus-based institutions. This has led to the UKOU often developing its own tools and systems, or making particular adaptations to them. A lot of the focus has been at the course, rather than institutional, level, for example specific simulations for a particular course. With large student numbers this sort of bespoke development can be justified, but one of the implications of e-learning has been a shift towards more centralized, institutional solutions.

The UKOU thus faced the sort of tension seen between revolutionaries and democrats, with most academics having been accustomed to developing their own specific tools, and thus acting in revolutionary mode, while as an institution the university recognized the need to make e-learning provision part of the mainstream and to offer a uniform quality of experience for students with regards to the technology they encountered on different courses.

In 2004 the UKOU initiated a VLE project. Because of its distance education mode of operation, a number of large-scale systems had been developed prior to the advent of VLEs. It was thus in the unusual situation of having developed or bought in a number of tools and systems that commonly constitute a VLE, without having these integrated into a recognizable VLE architecture. The question 'What VLE do you have?' could not be easily answered within the university. The tools it already possessed were:

- Discussion and conferencing – through OpenText's FirstClass system.
- Authentication – handled through an in-house system that allowed single sign on across all OU systems.
- Template driven content delivery – via an in-house XML based system.
- Blogging – available on some courses through the commercial software MovableType.
- Audio conferencing – Lyceum, an in-house product, had been successfully deployed on a number of courses, particularly in the study of languages (see Hampel and Hauck 2004).
- Assignment handling – a large-scale system had been developed in-house to match the UKOU's award process, including monitoring, final project handling and exam board processing.
- Assessment – a combination of the commercial package QuestionMark Perception and an in-house product, Open Mark, were used, although there was no enterprise solution, and practice varied.

In addition to these general services there was a wide range of software applications developed and deployed on single courses or within particular faculties.

As well as identifying areas where the existing provision could be improved, for example compliance with IMS Content Packaging for content delivery, the systems audit revealed a number of gaps, for example in terms of student tracking. What was perhaps most lacking, however, was the conception of these components as parts of a larger system.

Using the process set out in Chapter 5 a two-phase project was undertaken, the first part to determine the approach, the areas of development, the business case and strategy, and the second phase to implement the system, incorporating the staff development and cultural change issues. To recap, a six-stage process was detailed in Chapter 5:

1 Devise scenarios appropriate for your organization.
2 Engage in stakeholder consultation.
3 Perform an internal and external review.
4 Devise a set of general principles.
5 Draw up a feature list.
6 Map to strategic objectives.

Using the pedagogical approaches outlined in Chapter 3 and the different perspectives we saw in Chapter 5, a number of scenarios were constructed. These were used as the basis for an extensive stakeholder consultation process.

The stakeholder process was based around meetings with representatives from all the schools and faculties, tutors, students, library, technical staff, the university's commercial department, the group responsible for overseas partnerships and senior management.

In parallel an audit of the current system was conducted, which provided the list given above, as well as many smaller projects and tools, such as e-portfolios, which were in development. Although these systems were well known to all those engaged in the project, an audit from the perspective of creating an integrated VLE had not been conducted before. This process revealed a number of gaps, as well as overlap. In a large, distributed organization such as the OU, there are often a number of projects developed to meet the needs of a particular group, for example there were three separate e-portfolio projects under way, which were attempting to meet the needs of a particular course, professional development, and Ph.D. students. Similarly, there were two related, but still distinct, calendar projects, one of which was seeking to unify the various regional databases for the benefits of tutors and one to provide a tool for students. In both of these cases each project was aware of the others and they were seeking to establish a uniform approach, but lacked both the technical and the administrative means to do so. The VLE project thus acted as an umbrella under which such projects could proceed.

The external review looked at the standards work described in Chapter 7, the service oriented architecture approach, open source projects and commercial vendors.

A set of general principles was then devised. The function of these principles was to inform the decision making process for any tool, service or requirement that might form part of the VLE. They acted as a starting point for any requirement, and not as absolutes. For any one requirement there may be pedagogic, technical, performance or cost justifications for surrendering one or more of these principles. An example where a principle may be relaxed is where a client based tool is more suitable for technical or performance issues, but in such cases there is a trade-off, for instance in the portability of the solution or the integration of the service. The principles were:

- Learner-centric focus – the VLE should be viewed as a set of learning services and tools for learners, regardless of their current status with the university. This places the emphasis on providing tools for individuals, not courses. Thus most tools are available to the learner before, during and after they study a particular course. The course will then direct the student to use these in a particular manner (such as keep a blog on their studying), or configure them for use in the course (for example create specific asynchronous text conferences). This approach encourages users to view the OU VLE as their main online tool provider (even if they are not currently studying), encourages different types of learning (for example community-based, informal learning and complex learning over extended periods) and provides course/programme teams with a comprehensive baseline of online services from which to choose. There will be some course-specific developments (for example a simulation), which would not make sense at the general learner level, but the starting point should be to consider services as generic ones provided to all learners.

- Service oriented solutions – the VLE can be seen as a collection of services. Their actual level of integration into the VLE may vary, but in order for them to be easily adopted and implemented by course teams, they need to be available as a service, with standardized rules and set-up procedures. This involves creating solutions that can be called by different systems, are not 'hard-wired' into systems and can be readily replaced by new solutions.
- Delivery via the web – in order to achieve the objective of giving students access to the VLE from a range of locations and devices, the VLE needs to avoid client-based solutions wherever possible. It may be that occasionally a particular tool can only be, or is best, delivered via client software, but the potential difficulties this causes students needs to be recognized and the possible resultant lack of use of that tool that may arise. If web delivery is not possible, then thin clients that can easily be downloaded and installed should be investigated first.
- Delivery as a web service – in order to meet the objective of creating a future-proofed VLE and also a flexible one, the web services approach was recommended.
- Adoption of appropriate educational technology standards – in order to meet the objectives of creating a future-proofed system and facilitating partnerships, the adoption of educational technology standards is important, in particular Content Packaging, metadata, Enterprise and Learning Design specifications were seen as relevant.
- Adopt third party solutions where appropriate – one of the benefits of adopting a standards-based service oriented architecture is that it makes the adoption and integration of third-party solutions (theoretically) more achievable. Given this, the starting position when looking for any new tool was that a commercial or open source solution should be sought first, and only if these are deemed unsuitable would in-house development be undertaken.
- Security – transactions and data should be secure. The current authentication system needed some enhancement in order to work with VLE services provided by a third party, but such services should be capable of integration and not require separate logons.
- Accessibility – as an organization committed to openness, VLE services should be designed with accessibility in mind, and at a minimum conform to WAI (Web Accessibility Initiative) priority 1 and 2 guidelines.
- Administrative scalability – it is the deployment on a large scale that often distinguishes the UKOU's use of a technology from other uses of the technology. As well as performance issues (see Robustness), the

implications of this large-scale deployment are most keenly observed in the administrative demands. This includes being able to set up automatically a service for every student (compared with students setting up their own service), allowing different levels of access and permissions to that service (for example student, course team, tutor, system administrator), differential group management and applying policy (for example removing the service after a set period, dealing with unacceptable behaviour, etc). Any VLE service needs to be compliant with cost-effective administrative procedures, driven from UKOU systems such as the student records system.

- Consistency of user interface – in order to provide users with an integrated view and range of services, it is important that the user interface is consistent across all information feeds and services. This applies to the general design, but also to the function, presence, labelling and positioning of elements such as buttons and menus.
- Compliance with legislation – the VLE and its accompanying procedures should comply with all relevant legislation including data protection, disability discrimination, equal opportunities, human rights and freedom of information.
- Robustness and performance scalability – the VLE (and any service therein) needs to maintain performance reliability with a large number of users. It also needs to be robust so that users can perform a variety of actions (often unpredictable ones) without causing the service to fail.
- Centralized data ownership – tools and services should draw on centralized data sources and not store these locally.
- Usability – the VLE should be intuitive for all users to navigate. The design of each VLE component must take account of usability, to minimize the amount of user training needed. Training provision is costly, and likely to slow down adoption. The definition of each VLE service should include usability criteria and the goal-based and productivity measures that it should meet.
- Operational environment – all VLE services should ideally run on the UKOU's core operating systems (Windows, Linux and Solaris). In addition, all VLE server-side software should be capable of running on load-balanced servers, so that capacity can be increased as demand requires.
- Costs and savings – the VLE was not seen as a cost-saving exercise, particularly once procurement, development and training were taken into account. However, decision making about what e-learning elements and VLE services were to provide needed to take account of information on costs, both in terms of course production and presentation. It was deemed that the VLE should facilitate greater *clarity* in cost analysis and provide *opportunities* to reduce the costs of e-learning components without reducing quality, but we were careful not to make claims to particular savings.

Using the template described in Chapter 5 a set of functional requirements was then specified. Each of the functional requirements could be viewed as a project in its own right, and so the VLE role was to:

- act as an umbrella for this development;
- integrate the tools into a coherent framework;
- provide guidance and principles regarding development/deployment;
- provide direction and priority to development.

The requirements were grouped under five categories:

- personal functions;
- learning functions;
- learner support functions;
- course team functions;
- systems functions.

In total, 50 functional requirements were specified, some of which were already largely covered by existing tools, and others for which there was no provision.

Lastly these were mapped to the strategic objectives of the university. The UKOU also developed an e-learning strategy which had direct resonance with the VLE project. In addition the university had developed ten strategic directions, some of which directly influenced the VLE project, for example one such strategy was to strengthen leadership in modern pedagogy, and another was to promote partnership. From a VLE perspective these strategic directions favoured certain approaches; for example, in order to show leadership in modern pedagogy, an open source or service oriented approach was preferable to a commercial, proprietary solution, as it allowed flexibility in approach, and also demonstrated a degree of technical engagement with the VLE community. In order to promote partnership a VLE that operated to standards was important as this would facilitate partnerships in terms of exchanging content and data, without requiring both institutions to use the same systems.

Given that the OU VLE was not operating with a greenfield site, and the current trend was towards open architectures based around interoperability, then the logical solution to the OU VLE project was to view the current systems as a set of services that need to be integrated into an open architecture, in essence to impose an architecture upon previously disparate systems.

This had a number of benefits, both in the long and short term. In the short term it lessened the need to engage in large-scale staff development which a completely new system would necessitate. It also reduced the risk of systems failure, since all of the existing systems have been well tested. In the longer term it creates an architecture that will facilitate partnerships, at both the content and student data level. It also lessens the reliance upon any single system, since an open architecture based around standards facilitates the substitution of one system with another, as interactions between components are now performed via standard interfaces. It also provides a basis for incorporating new services as they become desired, provided they conform to certain principles. This will aid the support for pedagogic diversity and help future-proof the system.

However, although a service oriented approach was deemed the best choice, practical considerations led to the decision to adopt Moodle, for many of the reasons set out in Chapter 9. It provided a reasonable compromise between a completely in-house solution designed just for the institution and a commercial solution. The open architecture and code base of Moodle meant that existing systems such as the assignment handling and conferencing system could be incorporated into Moodle, while taking advantage of existing tools such as the assessment engine for generating quizzes. Strategically it was also felt that engagement with an open source community matched the UKOU's ideals.

State University of New York

The State University of New York (SUNY) has 64 campuses distributed over New York State. It also offers an extensive online programme through SUNY Learning Network, which has over 100,000 students, 3,000 staff and 40 of the campuses participate. Any VLE system therefore needs to support purely online, blended and campus based education, over a widely distributed system.

In 2005 they embarked on an extensive review programme to find the solution for their next generation VLE (having used the IBM Lotus Notes/ Domino system for a number of years). Their approach comprised four main stages (SUNY Learning Network 2005):

1 Assessments and assumptions – this established the foundational data that would be required of any VLE technology candidates. These reviews included technical and IT environment assessments, assumptions on requirements, and assertions for long-term trends in VLE development. The conclusions from this process were that the current system could no longer meet their needs and that a portal was 'the best technology foundation for a modern LMS'.
2 Analysis of task force recommendations – a task force made recommendations for a single VLE system across all campuses for teaching, learning, and research. The recommendations of that task force were then analysed in order to form the necessary criteria for evaluating

candidates for a new VLE solution. Five key evaluation criteria were then produced for use in the next stage:

(a) strong support for integration of new teaching and learning tools via open standards;
(b) student-centric rather than course-centric application design.
(c) support for the IMS Learning Design Specification.
(d) native interoperability with SUNY's portal environment.
(e) strong integration capabilities with campus IT systems.

3 Evaluation of potential solutions – using both the assessment studies and the analysis of the Task Force recommendations, potential solutions were evaluated. Once a strong solution had been identified, the team prepared an overview as well as a snapshot of a functional specification for production of that solution. The products they evaluated were Blackboard, WebCT, ANGEL, Academus, Moodle, Sakai, dotLRN, as well as the combinations of Sakai + Moodle + uPortal, Sakai + Academus + uPortal and Sakai + LAMS + uPortal. Their final recommendation was for a component approach, which combined uPortal, LAMS and a range of other open source tools, which they believe 'provides a much richer feature set than any currently available single-platform LMS'.
4 Implementation strategy – an implementation strategy for the proposed LMS solution was formulated. This is based around an 'agile' development plan with regular updates and some outsourcing of development.

The SUNY solution is summarized as 'a component strategy, as no single-platform LMS solution exists today to meet our needs. This powerful component strategy would integrate several carefully chosen open source projects, each with strong technical compatibility, resulting in a whole far greater than the sum of its parts' (SUNY Learning Network 2005: 5). This is unusual in a number of respects. First, it places the portal at the centre of the system, rather than a VLE. As we saw in Chapter 6, portals will be one of the technologies that vie for functionality with VLEs in the next few years, and SUNY have made the decision to prioritize the portal. Second, their process places a strong emphasis on the Learning Design specification we saw in Chapter 8, with it being one of the five key criteria that were used to determine the final system. This leads us on to the next noteworthy point about the SUNY solution, namely the selection of LAMS as their main VLE tool. While LAMS has gained a lot of attention and been successfully deployed in local contexts, it is rarely employed as the central system. The SUNY implementation will be an interesting test of how well LAMS manages this promotion to centre stage. The last point of note from the SUNY study is the conclusion of a component strategy, which, although based around uPortal and LAMS, also incorporates a number of best of breed components. This is exactly the open, standards based approach promoted by the service oriented architecture literature, and again the SUNY deployment will be a good test for the viability of this approach.

Deakin University

Deakin University is based in Victoria, Australia, with five campuses and approximately 35,000 students. It operates both campus and distance education courses, with around 15,000 distance learners. Like many institutions a number of VLEs had been adopted in different faculties, including TopClass, FirstClass, WebCT and Blackboard. As e-learning became more of a mainstream activity for the university, the need to centralize VLE provision and support became paramount. This was accelerated by top-down university policies, for example to make e-learning components compulsory in all awards and to have 10 per cent of their offering available purely online. E-learning was thus a key component in their overall strategy and an enterprise level VLE the means by which this would be realized.

In 2001 they decided to select a VLE that could replace their current varied provision. Their VLE decision making process was based around three areas of requirement (Smissen *et al.* 2003):

- Educational functionality – the system needed to match their teaching and learning functions over the next 3–5 years.
- Technical standards – the system needed to integrate with existing systems and work with their existing database and platform choices (Oracle and Unix respectively).
- Commercial viability – the vendor needed to be reputable, commercially viable and demonstrate a capacity to provide a high level of post-purchase service and support.

Each of these requirements formed a separate strand of the evaluation process, the result of which was a set of weighted selection criteria, which could be compared against a product short list. Their process was highly consultative, with numerous focus groups, a representative consultation group and web surveys of staff and students. From these a number of key features were established. These varied from general characteristics such as 'easy to use', to more specific tools, for example 'electronic assignment submission'. A further workshop was then used to weight each of the features, on a range of 0 – not important to 9 – essential, and these were compared between staff and students. Equipped with this functionality checklist they then engaged in detailed consultation with a short list of vendors.

They eventually selected WebCT, as they felt it met the functionality requirements better than any of its competitors and offered flexibility. Since 2003 they have implemented WebCT across all their campuses and the process has been largely successful, although as is always the case when moving from a poly-system to a mono-system, there was some resistance from users of other systems. The VLE team attribute this success to the transparency and inclusive nature of their process, and to the university-wide approach to technology integration.

New Zealand Open Source VLE project

Moodle was selected by the New Zealand Open Source VLE project to form the basis of their collaborative development. The project is a coalition of twenty tertiary education establishments in New Zealand who have committed themselves to using and developing an open source VLE. This is driven by a desire to share the costs of e-learning development. This made an open source option the most logical choice, so it was not a choice between open source and proprietary but rather a choice between open source alternatives.

Their objectives of the project are to (Wyles 2005):

- significantly reduce the total cost of ownership at a system wide-level;
- select and contribute to open source communities;
- encourage collaboration and user networks;
- reduce the barriers to entry: technology, support and professional development;
- accommodate flexible pedagogical approaches;
- support localization – including Maori and Pacific Island languages;
- be an advocate for interoperability;
- act as a catalyst for innovation.

They evaluated three open source options in detail: Moodle, ATutor and Ilias. They used two frameworks for their evaluation (Wyles 2004): Chickering and Ehrmann's (1996) seven principles of pedagogy and technology selection and Britain and Liber's (2004) framework for the pedagogical evaluation of eLearning environments.

They chose Moodle in 2004 because they felt that it offered:

- an open and active community with a critical mass of developers.
- a modular system architecture.
- relatively easy integration with other systems.
- a course/student focus rather than being tool-centric.
- adaptability.

Using Moodle as the basis, each of the participating institutions creates a distinctive and localized version. The second stage of the project is focusing on the development of additional tools such as a personalized portal, personal development planning (PDP) tools, e-portfolio, simulations and instructor support tools.

Conclusion

The four case studies in this chapter have all reached different conclusions regarding their VLE solutions, and it is worth considering to what extent the process itself predetermined the eventual solution. As I suggested in Chapter 5 the VLE evaluation process is not always as objective as those conducting it would like to believe. For instance, the process implemented at the UKOU and the one carried out at SUNY are similar in many ways in that they take a more fundamental approach, and tend to favour architectural solutions. Both the UKOU and SUNY reached similar architectural conclusions regarding the development of a service oriented approach around best of breed components, although the actual implementation of this varies at each institution. The process adopted by Deakin was more pragmatic in nature, for instance they immediately rejected any products that did not run on their existing database and operating system. They also placed ongoing technical support high on their list of priorities, whereas this is not mentioned at all for the SUNY and OU procedures. The conclusion of WebCT then is not surprising for Deakin, and similarly, by placing such an emphasis on Learning Design, the eventual choice of LAMS by SUNY can almost be viewed as inevitable.

Similarly, the choice between open source and proprietary options is often made upstream of a review of actual systems, even if this is only implicit. For the New Zealand project, the open source approach was seen as the key to their collaborative development effort. For the OU the open source influence was more subtle and reflected both technical and cultural values, but often these were not made explicit in the stakeholder consultation.

The type of processes set out here are all consultative in nature and usually take place over a reasonably extended time period. This can be frustrating for those who are enthusiastic about e-learning and want more rapid change. However, when viewed from an institutional perspective it is inevitable. In the next chapter we will look at this process of technology uptake in organizations, and also consider the broader picture of VLE adoption in higher education.

Chapter 13

Technology succession

In the previous chapter we looked at four case studies of VLE choice and implementation. It is useful to consider how representative these case studies are, so in this chapter we will look at current VLE uptake. We will also consider the process of technology succession, whereby systems and technologies come to be superseded by others.

Current VLE uptake

A 2004 survey conducted by the Organisation for Economic Cooperation and Development looked at e-learning in tertiary education in thirteen countries and a smaller survey by the Observatory of Borderless Higher Education reveal a good deal about the current situation regarding VLEs (OECD 2005). Nearly all institutions had a VLE of some description, but only 37 per cent of respondents had a single institution-wide VLE, while the remainder had a mixture of systems, often with one institutional and then a number local versions. However, 90 per cent expected to have an institution-wide system in the next five years. Just over half of the institutions used a proprietary system, often with some open source systems in conjunction. At the time of the survey, no institution operated solely with an open source system, although both the UKOU and the New Zealand project have since taken this route and were included in the study. Nearly half of the institutions had developed in-house solutions, which were often adaptations of open source or commercial systems.

The survey reinforces the perception gained from the case studies in this chapter, that actually it is not system functionality that influences choice, stating that

> there was little to choose between different systems. The past seven years of intensive LMS development and adoption in tertiary education have seen considerable system convergence. . . . Some respondents asserted that a particular system was the 'only genuine' enterprise LMS, or 'by far the easiest' to use, but it was difficult to evidence such claims
>
> (OECD 2005: 133)

As we saw in the case studies in the previous chapter, although the evaluation process will often focus on functionality, it is often other factors that influence the final decision. This is reflected in the explanation from McMullin and Munro (2004) at Dublin City University that the choice of an open source VLE was more aligned with the university's goal to become 'leaders in the development of effective learning technologies'.

The OECD survey seems to strengthen the position of commercial VLEs, but this may reflect the history of VLE uptake rather than its future direction. Three factors may see this position gradually undermined:

- Open standards – the development of open standards presents something of a dilemma for commercial VLEs. Customers expect the systems to comply with standards, and yet in doing so the commercial system begins to lose its unique selling point.
- Convergence of functionality – as system converge in terms of functionality, there is little to choose between commercial and open source options.
- Reliability of open source solutions – since 2004 a number of open source solutions have gained momentum to become serious rivals, most notably Sakai and Moodle.

Making predictions is a foolhardy enterprise, but if I were to guess at the findings of the next such survey, I would suggest four main conclusions:

- Nearly all institutions had moved to an institution-wide system. Initial VLE deployment happened at a local level, with different departments choosing systems based on their own preferences and needs. This historical position is partly reflected in the survey. However, as e-learning becomes part of the mainstream activity, this diversity of platform becomes unmanageable and institutions tend to settle on a single system.
- Few institutions operated an in-house solution. This is again a result of the need to mainstream activity. Initially in-house VLEs grew out of specific projects and research areas, but when these are required to operate at an enterprise level, the associated cost of maintenance and development becomes excessive.
- The VLEs will be divided equally between commercial and open source solutions. It is not that the market share of commercial solutions will necessarily decline, but open source solutions will meet the needs of many of those who currently operate in-house solutions, and provide a range of VLEs.
- Specialization and localization will occur through the use of services. Although there is a need in terms of support and resources to centralize the VLE service, this does not remove the initial differentiation between

departments that saw the adoption of different, local systems in the first stage of VLE uptake. There will be a demand for particular tools and services to meet the needs of specific subject areas or audiences, which won't be met by providing a different VLE, but rather by providing a different set, or configuration, of services within the institutional VLE.

Technology succession

Perhaps of greater interest is what the survey reveals about the other systems we saw in Chapter 6. Only 6.6 per cent of respondents reported an institution-wide content management system while 31 per cent reported an institution-wide portal, with a further 24 per cent expecting to implement one within a year. Compare these figures with the almost total adoption of VLEs (only one respondent reported no VLE).

What this demonstrates is that VLEs have achieved a level of uptake and penetration that has been rapid, but has not necessarily caused major disruptive changes. As we have seen, most VLEs seek to match current practice, certainly much more closely than a CMS, which as we saw in Chapter 6 requires a number of assumptions to be in place before it can be put to effective use. From this perspective then we can ask to what extent can VLEs be seen as a Trojan horse for other e-learning applications and practices that begin to more seriously change the nature of higher education? Portals and CMSs are, arguably, more significant change factors (whether for good or ill), but the VLE can be seen as the *sine qua non* for the implementation of such systems.

There is an analogy with the process of plant succession here. When there is a new environment, for example barren rock, a few pioneer species such as lichens begin to grow. The acid from these decomposes some rock particles, and their own death creates a coarse soil. This is suitable for mosses, which require little soil, and in turn these decompose to enrich and deepen the soil, until it is suitable for some grasses to grow. The process ends with the establishment of a stable, climax community. In e-learning terms, VLEs, and in particular commercial VLEs, have acted as the pioneer species, moving into the new environment and creating slight changes which make the habitat suitable for secondary colonizers. These might be seen as open source VLEs, or closely integrated systems such as portals and e-portfolios. The kind of environmental changes wrought by VLEs include general acceptance of the e-learning approach, integration with administrative systems, staff development, recruitment of enthusiasts, changes in assessment practice, acknowledgement of tools already used by students, and so on. Once these systems have been established, then the environment would be more receptive to systems that require more radical changes in practice, such as CMSs and PLEs.

Disruption versus succession

Christensen (1997) proposed the concept of disruptive technologies, which radically alter a market. The personal computer was one such example, disrupting and irrevocably altering the previous mainframe dominated computer market. While this is a powerful idea, it is sometimes given too much emphasis, with many people claiming that a new technology is disruptive, or that new technologies *should* be disruptive. For example blogs (Hiler 2002), open source software (Jackson 2003) and podcasting (Godwin-Jones 2005) have all been declared disruptive technologies. A technology is only disruptive if the broader market begins to use it in fundamentally different ways, and crucially that it appeals to a different audience than the existing technology. One cannot make or prescribe a technology to be disruptive. One could argue that far from being disruptive, blogs (to take one of the examples above) are simply a natural progression in the use of internet technology that relies on the previous steps being in place. Blogs are successful because they have built on the knowledge and skills users have acquired through interacting with and creating their own websites. They are not appealing to a different audience than these existing technologies, just offering them a development on their current technologies.

This over-emphasis on disruptive technology is akin to the genetic processes which underlie evolution – the great majority of evolutionary changes take place over a long period by the process of recombination, wherein subtle changes are made which make a slight difference. Mutation can cause large changes in genetic makeup and with it there are bursts along the evolutionary path, but these are by no means the main process at work. The same is true of technological change; disruptive technology, like mutation, is the more interesting, attention-grabbing process, but it is the slow, methodical process of technology succession, like recombination, which realizes most changes. So, while many technologies challenge the nature of practice in higher education, change is more likely to be brought about by the succession process outlined in the previous chapter than by revolutionary, disruptive changes.

Reshaping technologies

Marshall McLuhan (1962: 7) argued that 'technological environments are not merely passive containers of people but are active processes that reshape people and other technologies alike'. Although there is a whiff of technological determinism in this view that some may be uncomfortable with, what I feel is important is not the 'reshaping' of people, but the view of technology environments as *processes* and that technologies reshape other technologies. If one thinks of the adoption of a VLE as a process within higher education, and not 'merely' an implementation of technology, then its connection to the issues I set out at the start of this book become apparent. A VLE is both a means of achieving e-learning and a process through which we consider the role and nature of assessment in higher education (to choose but one example).

We might ask how technologies, and in our case VLEs, reshape other technologies? From a technological perspective the answer is twofold, relying on the competing forces of feature annexation and integration. The process of feature annexation we saw in Chapter 6 posits MLE sub-systems as being in competition for features, and thus VLEs will influence the functionality of associated systems such as e-portfolios as each seeks to establish a larger share in the MLE space by offering more features.

The second means of reshaping technologies is through integration. The process of integration is in some respects contradictory to that of feature annexation, although both can be in operation simultaneously, since feature annexation is a result of developers' actions and integration a goal of the individual institution. Integration seeks to bring varying systems closer together and thus they are required to interoperate smoothly, requiring some degree of collaboration, and also to offer complementary functions. The effect integration has on a technology is most apparent when two products announce a collaborative partnership, for example between the content management system HarvestRoad and the VLE Blackboard.

VLEs also reshape other technologies through human practices, which can either be top-down or bottom-up. Top-down directives include the creation of a specialized e-learning centre, a partnership with another institution, an e-learning strategy, or targeting a particular audience. Bottom-up influences include feedback or requests from students for particular features, frustration from educators with some features, successful implementation of e-learning programmes, enthusiasm from educators in using certain features, and so on.

The values of the net

Another way of looking at the uptake of technology is to view the internet as a social space and consider what values it seems to champion. This might cover questions such as:

- What are the social norms expected of behaviour when you join an online community?
- How are you expected to communicate?
- What is unacceptable behaviour?
- What sorts of topics generate online debate?
- What does the online community perceive as threats to its core values?
- Is there such a thing as one set of values for the internet?
- What sort of technologies take off online and why?
- How do people actually use the different technologies in everyday life?

To answer these questions it is necessary to consider the foundations of the internet and what it was created to achieve, namely communication, and in particular robust, decentralized and open communication. While these three (robustness, decentralization and openness) were *technological* features of the internet design, as the internet took off they also became *social* features of the system. A comparison of these two aspects of the internet, its technological and social features, reveals how each of these three key features is realized. In terms of robustness, the internet was designed as a distributed system that could survive attack, failure or sabotage of any particular part and still function as a meaningful communication system. In order to do this it had to be a network system, with no centralized control. This is fundamental to all that follows. Having opted for a decentralized system, this means that there needs to be many different connections, with no single node being more important than any other. This is realized through the network of internet routers, where if one is down, then information will simply find an alternative route. An open system follows from the decentralized approach, because if the system is to have no central control then it is necessarily open, so that any compatible computer can hook up onto it and allow communication to continue.

If we consider the internet in terms of social features and communication, these three key characteristics are evident again. Robustness is seen through the ability to communicate from different locations, using a variety of devices. It is also evidenced through the failure of governments or commerce to really control the internet and what is discussed on it. The decentralized nature of the internet is key to this – no one body or organization owns or controls the internet. Every server or website is potentially as significant as any other one. This makes the internet an obviously open and democratic place. Anyone can publish and debate is not governed or censored. In many ways, the internet acts like a living organism, driven by these social values. As John Gilmore famously observed, ‘the internet interprets censorship as damage and routes around it’. As well as making a strong case against censorship, what Gilmore’s quote indicates is that the social behaviour of the internet mimics the technological behaviour.

This provides an insight into the social values of the net and answers to the questions above. In short, the values of the internet are based around the sanctity of communication. Anything that appeals to these three key features of the net, namely openness, decentralization and robustness, is likely to take off online. Anything that threatens or impinges these is likely to cause concern and debate. This perspective on all internet developments, but especially those in e-learning, provides a useful means of both predicting what developments might be worth adopting, but also analyzing why certain technologies or approaches have been successful or unsuccessful. If one considers some of the successful internet technologies then they can all be seen as appealing to these three key features. For example, Napster, open source software, blogs and wikis can all be seen as being open (anyone can use and participate in them), decentralized (for example by pioneering peer-to-peer computing) and robust (consider the robustness of open source software such as Apache).

If we now consider current VLEs against these three features, then we can see that, although there is some correspondence, there is also a lot more that VLEs will need to do to match some of the technologies mentioned above. In terms of openness then the democratization role of VLEs has been significant so they have allowed many educators to easily create online courses, and in this respect are similar to blogs in terms of being open to all. From a technological perspective open source VLEs are obviously more open as the source code is available, although most commercial VLEs have application programming interfaces (APIs) that allow other components to plug into them. Even open source VLEs are closed in some respects, however, since they prescribe how tools need to be written to be incorporated into the core. A more open approach is one based around an open architecture where third party tools can be accommodated without them being written for or adapted for the system. We shall look at this more in the next chapter when we consider web 2.0 developments.

VLEs score reasonably well against the criterion of robustness, as all VLE developers have recognized that they represent a major enterprise system for universities and so need to be robust in terms of performance and security. The area of robustness that may be less valid is that of development, particularly concerning commercial VLEs. Microsoft potentially holds a warning for such companies here, with the new version of its operating system, Windows Vista, slipping from a projected 2003 delivery to a likely 2007 release. In the 1990s Microsoft shipped a new version almost every year, but as the software has become increasingly complex then so the ability to manage and control a project in the traditional manner seems to be inadequate. The same may apply to the proprietary approach to developing VLEs. A more robust model would be built around a decentralized, open source development approach, whereby a community can work on a number of smaller projects.

The key feature where VLEs do not score well is that of decentralization. As we saw in the discussion of PLEs, VLEs can be seen as an institutional response to e-learning, and as such centralization is at the heart of their deployment. As the OECD survey revealed, most institutions are moving towards a more, not less, centralized approach for VLEs. This gets to the heart of a key debate to be conducted in higher education and e-learning over the coming years, and that is to what extent universities provide a different, or specialized, environment. Currently most universities deploy tools that are specialized for use in education, with VLEs being the prime example, but also including portals and many bespoke applications. This is merely a reflection of the approach most campus universities take in the physical realm, where they provide students with their own accommodation, bars and restaurants which create an alternative environment to that of the conventional town or city where they reside. There are good reasons for copying this approach when it comes to the online world, such as support, quality assurance, resource allocation, and so on. However, as students become more technologically competent prior to entering higher education, they gather around themselves a number of applications. If one considers the types of tools we looked at in Chapter 4, then a student may have a blog, an instant messaging client, a voice over IP client (such as Skype), a range of social bookmarks, a Flickr photostream and a collection of information feeds. Taken as a whole these could represent an online learning environment, but the problem lies in compatibility with others, who may be using different tools.

Decentralization can also be seen as relating to content. Traditionally universities have acted as a repository of knowledge, with students having to physically come to this central location to acquire it. One area where VLEs have been effective is in promoting distance and flexible education, thus decentralizing the university to an extent. There is still a necessary emphasis on quality, but with a wealth of rich information available online it is increasingly difficult for universities to maintain a monopoly on content. What they will focus on is more about supporting and interpreting information, in aiding the process of knowledge creation from information, rather than acting as the source of information itself. As sites such as Wikipedia have demonstrated, good quality content can be created by a range of users, and for VLEs to fully support a decentralized model then they need to encourage this type of co-creation of content.

Conclusion

In the process of technology succession the significance of commercial VLEs can be realized. In Chapter 2 I listed some of the common complaints against current VLEs, including having a content focus, being based around a teacher–classroom model and not meeting the needs of different subject areas. However, if we view their adoption on a technology succession model, it is clear that they were successful precisely *because* of these perceived weaknesses. Because they match current practices closely they can be accommodated without the significant changes in practice that other systems, such as CMSs entail. If we return to our notion of revolutionaries and democrats then the process of succession again reveals the tension between these two groups. Revolutionaries would prefer to jump to the final stage, the climax community, whereas many democrats would prefer to maintain the current situation or at least progress slowly. The process of succession is the product of these two competing forces. The pace at which it proceeds will vary depending on the type of institution, the attitudes of staff, the needs of the learners, the input of senior management, and the technology choices.

The discussion around the three key features of the internet suggests some ways in which VLEs may develop, but also raises the question as to the extent to which universities continue to create a distinct experience for students. While they will continue to do so for many valid reasons there is also likely to be a shift towards recognizing and incorporating tools and content from elsewhere. The suggestion I made in the opening chapter that VLEs act as a proxy for many of the developments in higher education can be seen here. The trajectory of VLEs, and by extension universities, is towards a more open and decentralized model.

In the next chapter we will look at some current trends that will shape the direction of VLEs, and some research themes for VLEs over the coming years.

Chapter 14

VLE 2.0

While it is easy to create a fictional future populated by intelligent systems offering just in time education personalized to everyone's needs, there is always an element of science fiction about such predictions. What is probably more fruitful is to look at some current trends and developments in internet technologies and education and envisage how these would impact upon VLEs. In this chapter we will look at two such developments. The first is the open content movement, which is seeking to make educational content freely available online. The second is the concept of 'Web 2.0', which summarizes many of the current changes in internet technology. Given the institutional investment (both financial and human) in VLEs, and the conservative nature of higher education, developments in institutional university systems often lag behind those seen in the internet generally, and so by looking at the current trends we can extrapolate these on to VLE development over the next 5–10 years.

At the end of this chapter I will suggest some research strands for VLEs, which acts as a means of bringing together the themes and issues in the book.

Open content

Open content, or open educational resources (OER), is a simple enough concept – universities and similar institutions make their academic material freely available online for anyone to use. But, like so many seemingly simple ideas, it hides a wealth of complexity, and has profound implications for the way we conceive and practice higher education. Its nearest relation is the open source software movement, which we have looked at in detail already. While there are a number of similarities, and the open source approach provides a model for how open content may be realized, there are differences between (educational) content and software, and in particular between the educational and computer programming cultures that make it not simply a case of viewing open content as another form of open source.

Open content started in earnest with the MIT Open Courseware (OCW) initiative (http://ocw.mit.edu/index.html). This was started in 2001 through a grant from the Hewlett Foundation, with the aim of making all course materials available online. To date they have 1,400 courses, and in a one year period between 2003 and 2004 had 2.3 million visitors (Carson 2005). OCW constituted a very important statement. At a time when many universities and content providers were seeking to find ever more stringent methods of protecting their materials, OCW acted as an antidote to this and made people think about an alternative, open source based approach. It also caused serious debate about the nature of higher education and the business model of universities. If content was freely available, then would universities charge for accreditation and support? If so, these services could be offered by individuals or smaller institutions at a lower cost than those who also produce content. For MIT the release of their content could also be viewed as a statement of confidence, along the lines of 'We know there is more to an MIT qualification than just the content.'

Much of the MIT offering is in the form of course syllabuses, lecture notes, and some video material. This raised the question as to what type of content is best suited to the open content approach? It is easiest to release existing content, but often these only make sense in the context of a campus-based education, so at best they are of use to other lecturers, but not remote students. Content that was designed specifically for online delivery, what might be termed 'internet native' content, is preferable, but expensive to produce and not necessarily a natural by-product of what the university is doing. Any open content project that is designing material specifically for open content release, and not as part of the institution's daily operations, will only last as long as its funding.

If we are considering digital resources that can be used in different contexts, then this is also the basis of the learning object approach. A number of learning object repositories have also been created, almost in parallel to the open content work, and the two are now merging their efforts. So while they are not always labelled open courseware, there are a number of such repositories such as MERLOT (http://www.merlot.org/Home.po), which collect together reusable chunks of material.

The open courseware approach has generated a lot of interest globally, with US universities including Carnegie Mellon (http://www.cmu.edu/oli/index.html), UK initiatives including the UK Open University (http://oci.open.ac.uk/), the Japan OCW Alliance of universities (http://www.jocw.jp/), CORE, an organization that promotes open courseware amongst Chinese universities (http://www.core.org.cn/en/index.htm) and a large consortium of Spanish and Portuguese language universities (http://mit.ocw.universia.net/) all developing the idea and offering further content.

One of the criticisms of the open content approach is that it places the emphasis on content, and as educators are all too aware there is more to education than content. While it is true that content is not everything, that doesn't mean it is nothing. As I suggested in Chapter 1 the key to e-learning is to consider both the content and the dialogue aspects. By enabling them to locate and use high quality content, usually in combination with their own material, open content potentially frees up educators to concentrate on the element they have always added to education, namely support, interpretation and guidance.

Here we will consider the implications of open content for VLEs, and not for higher education in general. It raises some very fundamental questions for higher education, such as the development of sustainable business models, support, the role of universities in society and how accreditation is realized. For VLEs there are a number of implications that I can see:

- Raised profile for content management – we saw in the last chapter that the implementation of CMSs is still low compared with VLE uptake. An open content approach requires greater emphasis on content management, in terms of both content producers and content users, who may need to locate, store and adapt material. The assumptions we saw earlier regarding the use of CMS are more likely to be met if open content becomes significant for the majority of academics.
- A Learning Design emphasis – related to the issue of content focus mentioned above, one method of putting the pedagogy back into the open content world is to use Learning Design type approaches. This allows users to assemble resources and associate them with activities, rather than simply providing context-free resources. Activity sequences themselves are also reusable, providing a richer open content archive.
- A service oriented approach based on open standards – in order to make both content and designs reusable, they will need to remain neutral with regards to software tools. This would promote an open standards based approach and, to a lesser extent, a service oriented one also.
- Open source – in an open content community, it would be difficult to envisage proprietary systems being widely used, as the general ethos of openness, reuse and community development underpins the creation of such content.

VLEs and web 2.0

As a number of different applications and uses of the web began to become popular, there was a feeling that these represented a new phase of internet usage, one that was the result of the growing competence of users, the ubiquity of connection and the low cost of data storage. To encompass these new developments the term 'web 2.0' was coined, which has caught on rapidly, with many technologies and companies proclaiming themselves to be in some manner 'web 2.0' focused. So, what exactly is web 2.0? It can be seen as an umbrella term to describe some collective trends in the use of the internet. As such it may be a term that fades as quickly as it has risen, but for our purposes, particularly given the lag between general internet usage and institutional adoption through VLEs, it is a useful means of thinking about the challenges that VLEs will need to face over the coming years.

Web 2.0 is often specified in one of two ways – either as an approach, a way of thinking about the internet, or as a set of technologies that embody these principles. Although there is some debate as to who was responsible for the term, the publisher Tim O'Reilly is often associated with the term, and he clarifies what it means in *What is Web 2.0?* (2005).

In terms of applications then the following transitions all represent a shift from web 1.0 to web 2.0:

- Britannica Online → Wikipedia
- Personal website → blogging
- Mp3.com → Napster
- Content management systems → wikis
- Kodak/Ofoto → Flickr
- Netscape → Google

The web 2.0 version of each of these seem more participative, and this is one of the underlying principles, which O'Reilly teases out. The first of these principles is the notion of web as platform. This was an idea that first surfaced with much of the initial dot com hype. It challenged Microsoft, amongst others, because it suggested that the web browser essentially replaced the desktop operating system. In this view Netscape became the new Windows. That didn't come to pass, but O'Reilly suggests a crucial difference this time around, which is personified by Google. Whereas Netscape was based around a software product, Google is based around a service. He summarizes it thus:

> In each of its past confrontations with rivals, Microsoft has successfully played the platform card, trumping even the most dominant applications. Windows allowed Microsoft to displace Lotus 1-2-3 with Excel, WordPerfect with Word, and Netscape Navigator with Internet Explorer.
>
> This time, though, the clash isn't between a platform and an application, but between two platforms, each with a radically different business model: On the one side, a single software provider, whose massive installed base and tightly integrated operating system and APIs give control over the programming paradigm; on the other, a system without an owner, tied together by a set of protocols, open standards and agreements for cooperation.

Another principle, and one that has relevance for education, is that of 'harnessing collective intelligence'. Wikipedia is an obvious example here, as are many of the technologies we saw in Chapter 4. This ability to harness what James Suriowecki (2004) calls the 'wisdom of crowds' is partly what sets aside successful e-commerce sites such as eBay and Amazon. This seems to be one of the key principles, that users add value, and the technology or site needs to be set up so that it encourages participation. This shift to co-ownership of information and technology challenges the conventional hierarchical model found in traditional broadcast media.

In terms of software development web 2.0 applications operate a much more evolutionary model, continually adding new features and monitoring the use of these. Because the applications are all delivered online this can be achieved without the need for a major update and release of software. O'Reilly suggests that

> *Users must be treated as co-developers* . . . The open source dictum, 'release early and release often' in fact has morphed into an even more radical position, 'the perpetual beta,' in which the product is developed in the open, with new features slipstreamed in on a monthly, weekly, or even daily basis. . . .
>
> Real time monitoring of user behavior to see just which new features are used, and how they are used, thus becomes another required core competency. A web developer at a major online service remarked: 'We put up two or three new features on some part of the site every day, and if users don't adopt them, we take them down. If they like them, we roll them out to the entire site.'

Another principle is that of lightweight programming models. This includes the web services approach we saw in Chapter 7. The key to these models are that systems are loosely coupled, rather than tightly integrated. This facilitates the 'perpetual beta' model and also means that tools and services from other providers can be easily assimilated to make the overall system more powerful. The RSS method for syndicating information is also part of this approach and, as we saw in the section on portals, this allows different information sources to be assembled to make a personalized and customizable interface for a user. The approach is summarized as 'innovation in assembly', whereby value is added by assembling a number of different components together in a useful manner. This may have been achieved previously through hardware, for example Dell computers assemble components to produce PCs that suit a user's needs. With the sort of lightweight programming models now in practice, the same approach can be applied to tools and services.

O'Reilly finishes by summarizing the core competencies of web 2.0 companies, although not all of these are relevant to education:

- services, not packaged software, with cost-effective scalability;
- control over unique, hard-to-recreate data sources that get richer as more people use them;
- trusting users as co-developers;

- harnessing collective intelligence;
- leveraging the long tail through customer self-service;
- software above the level of a single device;
- lightweight user interfaces, development models, and business models.

Implications for VLEs

Having looked at the web 2.0 concept in general, we might now consider what the implications are for VLEs and e-learning, in short envisage a VLE 2.0. Just as web 2.0 can be framed both in terms of technology and mindset, so a VLE 2.0 can be considered from two perspectives. First, how would a VLE 2.0 be constructed, and second, what would VLE 2.0 education feel like? The two are not the same, and Downes (2006) has coined the term e-learning 2.0 particularly to refer to the latter. He asks

> What happens when online learning ceases to be like a medium, and becomes more like a platform? What happens when online learning software ceases to be a type of content-consumption tool, where learning is 'delivered,' and becomes more like a content-authoring tool, where learning is created? The model of e-learning as being a type of content, produced by publishers, organized and structured into courses, and consumed by students, is turned on its head. Insofar as there is content, it is used rather than read – and is, in any case, more likely to be produced by students than courseware authors. And insofar as there is structure, it is more likely to resemble a language or a conversation rather than a book or a manual.

Taking the technology aspect first, it seems fairly obvious to state that a VLE 2.0 would be based around a service oriented architecture, but there are a number of implications from this that are worth exploring. The concept of innovation in assembly is derived from the web services approach. This requires not only a technical adjustment, but also a cultural one, in how we develop and think of tools for use by students. The tendency up until now has been to develop tools that meet the specific needs of a course or set of students. The emphasis now is on developing tools that can be reused in different contexts and assembled in different ways.

The notion of 'perpetual beta' does not sit very well with some of the support and quality requirements of higher education, but it does suggest a method of VLE development. In this model, a new tool can be integrated in to the VLE, but only released to specific students. Following the evaluation of this, the tool is then made available to all students and academics. In this way the VLE becomes the conduit for new technologies, and accompanying good practice, that can be disseminated university-wide. The lightweight programming models and perpetual beta go beyond software development methodologies, however. As with the processes for selecting a VLE, these can be seen as embodying deeper values of the institution. Most higher education institutions will favour rigorous, consultative approaches when developing or adopting software with the specification process taking months and maybe years to complete, with the intention that the system will be in place for a suitably lengthy period. Such an approach does not match well with the faster, loose knit, rapid turnover mentality of the web 2.0 approach. Whether this conflict can, or should, be overcome will play a large influence in the direction of educational technology over the next few years.

A VLE 2.0 needn't necessarily be open source, although many of the principles are in line with the open source philosophy. What is more important is that it is an open architecture, based around standards, so that the sort of easy coupling and decoupling of tools mentioned above can be accomplished. It is likely, however, that a VLE 2.0 is much less of an 'out of the box' entity than current VLEs, as it will be constituted from a range of tools and services and configured differently for different users. It is unlikely that all of these components will come from one provider – some may be commercial products, others open source and still others in-house solutions. Given their open approach a number of these services will be from outside the educational sector, for example by incorporating Google or Flickr tools into a VLE. Users will become increasingly unable to determine that they are using a different application, as these can be adapted to meet the needs of the institution.

Although the VLE is likely to be an institution-wide one, as we saw in the previous chapter, localization and adaptation can be realized through a service oriented approach, and is in keeping with the web 2.0 principle of lightweight assembly. Thus the medical school in a university may have a different configuration of tools than the business school, but both are using the same underlying VLE. Some of the approaches to personalization we saw in Chapter 10 and in the section on portals will add to this increased sense of heterogeneity in VLE experience. However, the web as platform principle does seem to undermine the desktop-based client approach proposed by some, and the browser is likely to remain the dominant interface.

The portal approach to assembling information and tools seems more in keeping with the web 2.0 principles, with increased emphasis on the sort of MyUniversity space we saw in Chapter 6. In terms of VLEs then this may see portals occupying a more central role in the overall MLE, or VLEs becoming more portal-like in their operation.

Increased surveillance and monitoring of use is concomitant with the principle of harnessing collective intelligence and the perpetual beta development cycle, since it is important to know general patterns of use. As we saw in the chapter on personalization, there are a number of negative pedagogical and privacy implications associated with monitoring student behaviour.

In terms of the impact upon educational practices, the principle of collective intelligence is probably the most significant. This could be realized in a number of ways, but at its core is the idea of students as co-creators of content. This could be in terms of creating chunks of content that populate a resource pool, or in making course content available in a wiki so students can modify it, allowing students to mark up content and create shared bookmarks, and so on. The content thus evolves over subsequent presentations as each cohort modifies it. In Chapter 1 I gave the example of how e-learning often led people to rethink assessment strategies, and in a web 2.0 version of e-learning the practice of peer assessment would become more prevalent as it reflects this notion of collective intelligence.

Another principle that has wider implications is that of reuse, which is inherent in the web 2.0 way of working. In terms of applications this means reusing tools and components, but once reuse is common practice, the same may apply to content also. As we have seen there are a number of learning object repositories and open content initiatives which similarly seek to promote reuse. In the chapter on standards I mentioned that the initial focus had been on content and then it had shifted to tools and learning designs. It may be that this was the reverse of what actually needed to happen, and reuse of content is more likely to occur once the culture of reuse has been established through reusing and assembling software components. The innovation in assembly principle could apply equally well to content. As O'Reilly says, 'the Web 2.0 mindset is good at re-use'.

Just as web 2.0 applications have much less rigid boundaries than conventional software, so might a web 2.0 educational experience. This would be seen in content initially; it would pull content in from different providers, without the user being aware of where it actually resided. It might also be seen in the types of support students receive, for example instead of one educator providing support across the length of a course, they may provide support for certain elements across multiple courses. This represents a vertical, rather than horizontal, slice through the support process. This would be facilitated through web 2.0 applications that offer specific support within content, for example embedded text, real-time chat, video or audio conferencing.

The VLE 2.0 concept is summarized in Figure 14.1.

VLE research directions

Before concluding this chapter and the book, I would like to draw together some of the themes we have covered by considering a possible research agenda for VLEs over the next five to ten years. Obviously within this period there will be unexpected developments and new technologies. Ten years ago VLEs themselves weren't really in existence, but even so it was possible to consider the implications of the internet for education, and while some of

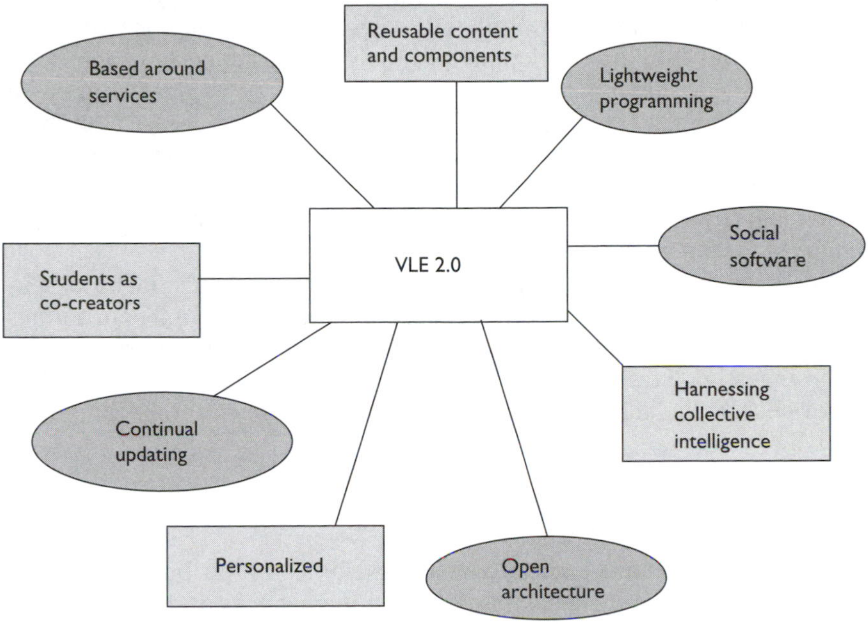

Figure 14.1 VLE 2.0.

the initial hype surrounding e-learning was unfounded, there were issues raised at that time which higher education is only now coming round to acknowledging. Five years ago there were not many viable open source VLEs, but trends from outside education would have suggested that they would become a potent force, and that the move would be towards institution-wide systems. While some of the suggested themes here may not turn out to be significant then, and others may be superseded by other developments, enough of them will tax educational technologists and those in higher education over the coming years.

Personalization

This is one of the real strengths of e-learning, in that it potentially provides a means of offering a degree of personalization to users, so that their education better suits their needs. This is possible without e-learning technologies – the Oxbridge model of intensive one-to-one tuition is the ultimate in personalization, but this is not a scaleable model. Given the global expansion in student numbers over the past decade the trend is more towards large-scale courses with packed lecture halls than towards intimate tutorials. If you are one of a few hundred attending a lecture it does not feel like a very personalized experience. A VLE that provides material suited to your needs, information based on your preferences and a community based around your interests would feel more tailored towards the individual. Therefore one strand of research will be on the development of tools that foster such an approach. This could be in the form of content repositories that allow greater variety in content provision, or configurable PLEs. It could also be tools that contribute to a more flexible environment; for example Buddyfinder is an extension to instant messaging that allows users to log their interests or expertise, so if an individual required help with a subject they could use the tool to find people online at that moment who could offer advice.

However, as we saw in Chapter 10, personalization should not be seen as an unalloyed force for good within education. There are a number of serious questions surrounding personalization, and a separate strand of research would be to investigate the effects of personalized environments on the student experience, including the impact of surveillance and any loss of identity with the cohort.

Affordances and mediating artefacts

One dilemma we have encountered several times in this book is that the complexity required by technology to meet the nuances of the educational process effectively renders the technology unusable by non-experts. E-learning approaches only really become significant when they cease to be specialized areas of research interest and become common practice. This has been where commercial VLEs have been successful, through a combination of ease of use and close alliance with everyday practice. However, as has been noted there are drawbacks to simply mimicking current practice, as this neither takes advantage of the benefits e-learning offers, or provides as good an experience as the face-to-face version it copies.

While this was adequate for a first generation of e-learning, as we move towards a second generation then there is a need to move beyond these approaches. This is where affordances can come into use. By designing tools specifically to provide e-learning affordances for educators then VLEs which are both easy to use and promote pedagogy that is better suited to online study can be developed.

Affordances, patterns and learning design can all be seen as forms of mediating artefacts, which act as intermediaries between educators and technologies. The use of such artefacts is likely to increase and so research into both new forms of artefacts and also their effectiveness is required.

Service oriented approaches

The sections on open content and web 2.0 both indicate a future where service oriented approaches are commonplace. In fact a service oriented approach and mind set is almost a prerequisite for these developments. However, while some initial steps have been made towards implementing SOA as the basis of a VLE, a fully service oriented approach is far from the norm. Thus the first strand of research will be to continue to extend this work. This will be in terms of developing the sort of generic tool descriptions we saw in Chapter 9, creating tools that have an SOA basis and reconfiguring institutional as services that can be assembled.

There is something almost aesthetically appealing about the concept of service oriented architectures, that may result in educational technologists being seduced by the idea without analyzing them rigorously. A further strand of research then needs to address the benefits and drawbacks of this approach from a number of perspectives, including efficiency, robustness, user experience, development and maintenance costs, and security.

The research strands outlined here have a good deal of overlap and commonality and a number of them are predicated on a service oriented approach, which is by no means a certainty. A critical approach is necessary, which is why research is required both in the development of such approaches, but also in their effectiveness. It could be that in ten years time we talk about SOA with the same nostalgia we now discuss virtual reality with, but my guess is that even if the term fades, the essence of it, the loose coupling and perpetual release cycle, will become mainstream.

Reuse

Given much of the impetus, funding and research in the area, one could be forgiven for thinking that reuse is a commonplace activity in higher education. This is not the case, except perhaps at an informal level. The fact that it makes sense to reuse content for both the educator, who does not need to spend their time specifying all their material, and the student, who gets high quality resources, is not sufficient to overcome some of the barriers to reuse. Part of this is wrapped up in professional identity, with many educators feeling that it is their role to create all their content. This may be viable if we are talking about lecture notes, but becomes increasingly difficult with e-learning. This gets us to the heart of the issue – reuse becomes practice when it produces significant savings in terms of time, people or money. For example, producing lecture notes is relatively low intensity work, particularly if you are building on previous presentations. The natural tendency is always to create your own material, since it will best fit your needs, so the potential benefit gained from reuse is never sufficient to make it common practice. A highly interactive e-learning course with multimedia and collaborative activities, however, is a much more resource intensive production task. The benefits of reuse become sufficient then to overcome the do-it-yourself threshold.

This return on investment is more pronounced with software and so reuse of components is worthwhile. There is also a culture among programmers of reusing software components, which is not found amongst educators. VLE research on reuse will need to focus on the granularity of components that are reused, for example is it at the level of pieces of code, or whole applications? The effort required to reuse components will also need to be researched, so the level of adjustment required to make a tool work within your system can be gauged against the cost of simply developing one from scratch. From a technical perspective further tools and, more importantly, methods for integrating components will need to be developed and tested.

In terms of reusing content, the open content and learning object initiatives need to establish a critical mass of resources so that any individual searching for a topic will have a range of resources to choose from, and is thus more likely to find one that meets their needs. The type of granularity is important here also – do users prefer to reuse assets, learning objects or whole courses? The manner of reuse and degree of reversioning required will also influence the nature of VLEs, for example if reuse is found to be most useful in personalization then VLEs will need to accommodate this. Research will also need to further develop tools that facilitate searching across a range of distributed collections, and pulling resources in to the VLE, while recording rights and permissions for usage.

Negotiation of the MLE space

As we saw in Chapter 6, there are a number of different systems that constitute the overall MLE for an institution. Many of these systems are competing for features and primacy within the overall MLE space. This competition is as much (if not more) political as it is technological, as different groups may have interests in particular systems. A move to the type of loosely integrated systems specified in the web 2.0 vision of technologies encourages this type of competition, since systems can be broken down into constituent services. Thus one package may offer a number of services which can be used in different areas. This type of loose coupling also blurs the boundaries between systems, and the assembly approach makes these boundaries much more permeable. Thus increasingly what constitutes a VLE, a portal, or CMS will be difficult to say; it is much less likely that you can name your specific product for these, but rather they are created through the assembly of a number of components.

The research in this area that will be fruitful is the technical process of building such component systems, and modifying constituent elements. There is also an interesting strand on the institutional and organizational practices that influence such decisions, which addresses the political and cultural perspectives that the final MLE personifies. Lastly, the way we think about such systems needs addressing, as I suggested in the section on metaphors in Chapter 6. With much looser coupling and less rigid boundaries, the current architectural and engineering models may not be appropriate.

Education business models

As well as blurring the boundaries between systems, a web services approach blurs the boundaries between roles within education also. In the section on open content I mentioned that the component parts of education could become unbundled in a world where good quality content was freely available. With a variety of monitoring and support tools, then the type of support offered to students could also be subject to change, for example on a per query basis. If content is not free, then licensing for use with automatic payment may also be another model. One could imagine an Amazon-like site populated with learning objects, which could be purchased for a flat fee, along with all the Amazon-type features, such as recommendations ('People who bought this learning object also purchased this one . . .'), reviews, lists and even new features such as learning pathways that compile a set of resources into a course.

Another area of change in business practice may be in the technical area. If open source software and open standards prevail, then it is not software that becomes valuable, but expertise. There will be increasing demand for consultants who are 'IMS certified' or 'Sakai approved', who can perform the complex task of integrating the various components in an MLE.

Other areas of change might include the provision of different types of study to meet the needs of lifelong learners, and a different relationship with alumni, by providing them with services such as e-portfolios, portals, blogs, etc. which builds a long-term relationship with the university.

My aim here is not necessarily to propose these business models as superior or desirable; one has visions of an academic call center with professors sitting around answering phones on a commission basis, while an overseer prowls the floor. But most businesses have had to adapt to the changes wrought by the internet, and often for the better from a consumer perspective. By researching the institutional impact of such technologies on educational practice it is possible to devise models that utilize the benefits of the technology and work to the advantage of students and educators.

E-learning pedagogy

As we move beyond the first wave of VLE use, which sought to replicate much of common practice, the next phase of e-learning is likely to be more adventurous. This is likely to occur through a combination of familiarity and comfort with using internet technologies, and tools that aid the educator in doing so. In other words, through the processes of technology succession and affordances. The first strand of research in this theme then will be to continue existing research in to the effectiveness of different pedagogies and the learner experience of these. How educators develop e-learning courses, and the associated staff development requirements, will also be part of this research.

Another strand will be in the development of means of sharing such practices, which could be through the use of Learning Design type approaches, or representations such as patterns. Easy reuse and sharing will ease the process of creating effective e-learning activities.

A final area of research in this strand will be to develop the kind of tools that aid educators in developing engaging e-learning activities, without requiring them to gain expertise in the area.

Shifting boundaries

The final research area for VLEs I have termed shifting boundaries because it examines the manner in which current distinctions will be blurred or redefined as VLEs develop. For example, although virtual in nature, current VLEs require the use of PCs, which limits the study space for learners. Various developments in mobile learning will begin to remove some of these restrictions. This is seen with the use of wifi access in public places, so learners are not restricted to their specified study location. It is further altered by the provision of information and content in different formats so they can be accessed on a variety of portable devices. Mobile learning significantly blurs the boundary between the classroom and the external environment, for example Sharples (2003) recounts how school children used mobile devices that were preloaded with information to research canals on a field trip. They recorded their findings with the devices, which they then brought back to the classroom to create presentations.

A similar distinction that is becoming less relevant is that between formal and informal learning. The advent of technologies such as e-portfolios can be seen as an attempt to recognize, even legitimize, informal learning. The use of more socially oriented tools we saw in Chapter 4, and which typify web 2.0, also promote informal, peer driven dialogue. Related to this is the distinction between types of content. With so many information sources available there is less emphasis on the academic to provide all of the content themselves, so as long as the content is appropriate, where it comes from is less important.

Another boundary that becomes less significant is that between tools and content. In Chapter 1 I suggested that e-learning is often divided in to the broadcast and discussion models, to the detriment of both. In a lighter, service oriented approach this distinction becomes less relevant. For example Netvibes (http://www.netvibes.com) provides an individual portal that mixes content in the form of RSS feeds, and tools (for example email, to do lists) within the same interface.

For higher education institutions perhaps the most significant boundary is that between the institutions themselves and this is one area where VLEs could be very significant. The development of the standards we saw in Chapter 7 makes these boundaries significantly more permeable, so students could be taking courses from more than one university, or be studying with one university but have content provided by another.

There are undoubtedly other boundaries that will be affected by, and in turn will affect, VLEs, and so research that both evaluates the impact of these boundary changes and aids their redefinition will help construct a view of higher education as a whole.

Conclusion

All of this raises the question as to whether a VLE 2.0 will be a VLE at all. The process of technology succession we saw in the last chapter suggests that the future of the VLE is probably one of gradual change (although 'gradual' is relative; in internet terms it may seem slow, but by the more glacial time frames found in higher education it will seem like a rapid change). This is likely to happen in two directions simultaneously. The first will be outward facing as VLEs assimilate new tools into their standard tool set – for example it won't be long before all VLEs incorporate the tools listed in Chapter 4 as a default. The second direction is backward into the institution, and will involve architectural and technical development, towards the more service oriented, loose integration we have encountered.

What is interesting for the VLE as a separate entity is what happens when these two developments have reached a level of maturity. A VLE will consist of a number of tools that may come from a range of different providers, each of which can be decoupled easily. Users will be accustomed to using their own tools, and the distinction between content and tools has been eroded. In this scenario a learner's environment is more akin to a portal with a collection of tools and content, some of which are provided by the institution and others by external parties. The VLE ceases to be a convenient term or concept at this stage. So, one could argue that, rather like the male praying mantis, the ultimate sign of the VLE's success is its own demise.

Appendix: Activity used in Learning Design

Technology viewpoints: Background

The way people react to the internet is often influenced by an underlying view of that technology (or indeed all technology). Some perceive the internet as a threat, to their status, career, values they hold dear or aspects of society in general. Even if these underlying beliefs are not articulated or even acknowledged they will inform the type of activity such a person views the internet as being suited for. For example, if someone's underlying assumption was that the net is a detrimental force in society they might think of it as essentially a distribution medium for pornography. Conversely, others may see the internet as a revolutionary force that empowers individuals by allowing the free exchange of information.

Such viewpoints might be termed dystopian and utopian respectively. Technological utopias and dystopias are frequently found in science fiction, where the author, wishing to make a comment on current society, envisages a future society where technology has either freed or enslaved human beings (for dramatic purposes, the latter is usually preferable). However, examples of such views are not only to be found in science fiction. Educational technology literature over the past 20 years shows the promises and fears that have been associated with a variety of technologies including computers, CD-ROM, computer assisted learning, artificial intelligence, virtual reality, videodisc, etc. The internet is just the latest in this list.

What both the positive and negative viewpoints have in common is that they see the technology itself as shaping human behaviour. The term for this is 'technological determinism', a phrase first coined by Thorstein Veblen, and elaborated upon by Marshal McLuhan. The technological deterministic viewpoint is that technology is an autonomous system that affects all other areas of society. Thus human behaviour is, to a greater or lesser extent, shaped by technology.

The contrary view is called 'social determinism' which, put simply, claims that society is the controlling factor. Thus society shapes how individuals behave and also how technology is used within that society.

This grid combines these two continuums:

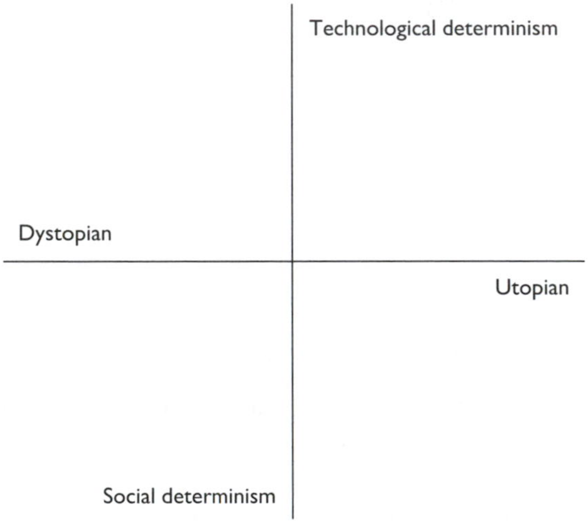

Activity 1

In this activity you will be determining your own beliefs regarding technology. Firstly, read the following material, which covers technological and social determinism, to gain a deeper understanding of the concepts.

Technological determinism. http://www.umsl.edu/%7Erkeel/280/tecdetrm.html

Chandler, D. (1996) *Shaping and being shaped*. *CMC Magazine*, 1 February 1996. http://www.december.com/cmc/mag/1996/feb/chandler.html

Kling, R. (1996) *Hopes and horrors: technological utopianism and anti-utopianism in narratives of computerization*. *CMC Magazine*, 1 February 1996. http://www.december.com/cmc/mag/1996/feb/kling.html

Chandler, D. *Technological or media determinism*. http://www.aber.ac.uk/media/Documents/tecdet/tecdet.html

Now place your own personal view of the internet on the grid above. Justify your positioning by providing examples of how you view the Net and the sort of stories regarding it that interest you.

Activity 2

Read the following articles and chapters and place each on the grid above, justifying your positioning.

Weller, M. (2002) *Delivering Learning on the Net,* Chapter 1

Noble, D. (1997–2001) *Digital Diploma Mills* (There are several articles under this collective heading. There is no need to read all of them, one will suffice, although you may like to read them all.) http://communication.ucsd.edu/dl/

Spender, D. (1998) *Building up or dumbing down, A Keynote Address to the Communities Networking/Networking Communities Conference*. http://gos.sbc.edu/s/spender1.html

Kling, R. (1996) 'Computerization at work'. *CMC Magazine*, August 1996. http://www.december.com/cmc/mag/1996/aug/kling.html

References

A'Herran, A. (2000) 'Research and evaluation of online systems for teaching and learning', *AusWeb2k-The Sixth Australian World Wide Web Conference*, Rihga Colonial Club Resort, Cairns, 12–17 June 2000. http://ausweb.scu.edu.au/aw2k/papers/a_herran/paper.html

Adler, C. and Rae, S. (2002) 'The future of e-learning is learner-centric', *LTI Newsline*, 1 Jan 2002. http://www.elearningmag.com/ltimagazine/article/articleDetail.jsp?id=6687

Ahmed, O. (2005) *Migrating from Proprietary to Open Source Learning Content Management Systems*. Thesis, Department of Systems and Computer Engineering, Carleton University. http://eduforge.org/docman/view.php/7/414/Owais_Ahmed_TTMthesis.pdf

Alexander, C. (1979) *The Timeless Way of Building*. Oxford University Press.

Alexander, C., Ishikawa, S., Silverstein, M., Jacobson, M., Fiksdahl-King, I. and Angel, S. (1977) *A Pattern Language: Towns, buildings, construction*. Oxford University Press.

Alvardo, P. (2004) 'Seven steps to selecting a learning management system', *Chief Learning Officer,* January 2004. http://www.clomedia.com/content/templates/clo_webonly.asp?articleid=365&zoneid=78

Amis, M. (2003) *Yellow Dog*. Jonathan Cape.

Automatic Metadata Generation (2006) http://www.cs.kuleuven.ac.be/~hmdb/amg/index.php

Bales, R. F. (1950) 'A set of categories for the analysis of small group interaction', *American Sociological Review* 15 pp. 257–63.

Becta (2004) ICT and e-learning in Further Education: Embedding technology, evolving practice. A summary of the report to the Learning and Skills Council. http://ferl.becta.org.uk/content_files/pages/surveys/monitoring%202004/ILT%20survey%20summary.pdf

Becta (2005) *Open Source Software in Schools.* http://www.becta.org.uk/corporate/publications/documents/BEC5606_Full_report18.pdf

Beierle, T. C. (2002). 'The quality of stakeholder based decisions', *Risk Analysis* 22(4) pp. 739–49

Bergin, J. (2000) *Fourteen Pedagogical Patterns*, http://csis.pace.edu/~bergin/PedPat1.3.html

Bergquist, M. and Ljungberg, J. (2001) 'The power of gifts: Organizing social relationships in open source communities', *Information Systems Journal* 11 pp. 305–20.

Black, P. and Wiliam, D. (1998). 'Assessment and classroom learning', *Assessment in Education* 5(1) pp. 7–71.

Blood, R. (2000) *Weblogs: A history and perspective*. http://www.rebeccablood.net/essays/weblog_history.html

Boyle, E. (2002) *CETIS EC-SIG Content Exchange Evaluation Report*, CETIS. http://www.cetis.ac.uk/groups/20010809144711/FR20020301142909

Boyle, T. and Cook, J. (2004) 'Understanding and using technological affordances: A commentary on Conole and Dyke', *ALT-J, Research in Learning Technology* 12(3) pp. 295–9.

Braganza, C. (2006) *LAMS Tool Contract*. http://wiki.lamsfoundation.org/display/lams/Tool+Contract

Brake, D. (2005) *Korean Blogging is Huge!* 20 January 2005. http://groupblog.workasone.net/archives/2005/01/korean-blogging-is-huge/

Britain, S. (2004) *A Review of Learning Design: Concept, specifications and tools*, JISC. http://www.jisc.ac.uk/uploaded_documents/ACF83C.doc

Britain, S. and Liber, O. (2004) *A Framework for the Pedagogical Evaluation of elearning Environments*. http://www.cetis.ac.uk/members/pedagogy/files/4thMeet_framework/VLEfullReport

Brown, T. and Jenkins, M. (2003) VLE Surveys: A longitudinal perspective between March 2001 and March 2003 for higher education in the United Kingdom. http://www.ucisa.ac.uk/groups/tlig/vle/index_html

Bruner, J. S. (1996) 'Frames for thinking: Ways of making meaning'. In Olson, D. and Torrance, N. (eds) *Modes of Thought: Explorations in culture and cognition*, pp. 93–105, Cambridge University Press.

Butler, T. R. (2002) 'Pouring over the facts: Andreas Pour on KDE', 21 August 2002, *Open for Business*. http://www.ofb.biz/modules.php?name=News&file=article&sid=158

Carson, S. (2005) *MIT OCW Evaluation Findings*. http://ocw.mit.edu/NR/rdonlyres/90C9BC91-7819-48A0-9E9A-D6B2701C1CE5/0/MIT_OCW_2004_Program_Eval.pdf

Chickering, A. and Ehrmann, S. C. (1996), 'Implementing the seven principles: Technology as lever', *AAHE Bulletin*, October, pp. 3–6. http://www.tltgroup.org/programs/seven.html

Chohan, N. (2001). 'VLE procurement', *JISC Briefing Paper No. 2*. http://www.jisc.ac.uk/mle/reps/briefings/bp2.html

Christensen, C. M. (1997) The Innovator's Dilemma: When new technologies cause great firms to fail. Harvard Business School Press.

Cole, J. (2005) Using Moodle: Teaching with the popular open source course management system. O'Reilly.

Conole, G. (2006) 'The role of "mediating forms of representation" in Learning Design', *Networked Learning Conference 2006*, Lancaster, UK. http://www.networkedlearningconference.org.uk/abstracts/pdfs/P32%20Conole.pdf

Conole, G. and Dyke, M. (2004) 'What are the affordances of information and communication technologies?' *ALT-J, Research in Learning Technology* 12(2) pp. 113–24.

Counterman, C., Golden, G., Gollub, R., Norton, M., Severance, C. and Speelmon, L. (2004) *Technical Report Sakai Project: Sakai Architecture v1.0* http://cvs.sakaiproject.org/release/1.5.1/docs/Sakai-Architecture-1.0.0.pdf

Dalziel, J. (2005) 'From reusable e-learning content to reusable learning designs: Lessons from LAMS', *EDUCAUSE AustralAsia*, Auckland, 5–8 April2005. http://www.lamsfoundation.org/CD/html/resources/whitepapers/Dalziel.LAMS.doc.

Davies, N. J., Fensel, D. and Richardson, M. (2004) 'The future of Web Services', *BT Technology Journal* 22(1) pp. 118–30.

Dean, K. (2000) 'Instant messaging grows up', *Wired Magazine* 25 Jan 2000. http://www.wired.com/news/culture/0,1284,33736,00.html

Downes, S. (2006) 'E-learning 2.0', *Elearn Magazine*. http://elearnmag.org/subpage.cfm?section=articles&article=29–1

Drozdik, S., Kovács, G. L., and Kochis, P. Z. (2005) 'Risk assessment of an open source migration project', *Proceedings of First International Conference on Open Source Systems*, Geneva, pp. 246–9.

EduTools (2006) 'CMS: Product List'. http://www.edutools.info/item_list.jsp?pj=8

Egan, K. (1988) *Teaching as Storytelling: An alternative approach to teaching and curriculum in the elementary school*. Althouse Press.

Evans, P. and Wurster, T. S. (2000) *Blown to Bits: How the new economics of information transforms strategy*. Harvard Business School Press.

Fisher, W. R. (1987) *Human Communication as Narration: Toward a philosophy of reason, value and action*. University of South Carolina Press.

Foucault, M. (1979) *Discipline and Punish: The birth of the prison*. Penguin.

Free Software Foundation (2003) Various licenses and comments about them. http://www.fsf.org/licenses/license-list.html.

Fricke, A. and Voelter, M. (2000) 'Seminars: A pedagogical pattern language about teaching seminars effectively', *Proceedings of EuroPLoP2000*. http://www.voelter.de/data/pub/tp/tp.pdf

Gall, M. and Breeze, N. (2005) 'Music composition lessons: The multimodal affordances of technology', *Educational Review* 57(4) pp. 415–33.

Gamma, E., Helm, R., Johnson, R. and Vlissides, J. (1995) *Design Patterns: Elements of reusable object-oriented software*. Addison-Wesley.

Gaver, W. W. (1991) 'Technology affordances'. *CHI'91 (Conference on Human Factors in Computing Systems)*, New Orleans, 28 April–2 May 1991.

Gibson, J. J. (1979) *The Ecological Approach to Visual Perception*, Lawrence Erlbaum.

Goddard, A. (1998) 'Facing up to market forces'. *Times Higher Education Supplement*, 13 November.

GNU (1991) GNU General Public License. http://www.gnu.org/copyleft/gpl.html

Godwin-Jones R (2005) 'Skype and podcasting: Disruptive technologies for language learning', *Language Learning & Technology* 9(3) pp. 9–12. http://llt.msu.edu/vol9num3/emerging/default.html

Goodyear, P., Avgeriou, P., Baggetun, R., Bartoluzzi, S., Retalis, S., Ronteltap, F. and Rusman, E. (2004) 'Towards a pattern language for networked learning', *Proceedings of Networked Learning 2004*, pp. 449–55. http://dspace.ou.nl/bitstream/1820/301/2/paperNetworked+learningconferencepatternlanguage.doc

Green, H., Facer, K., Rudd, T., Dillon, P. and Humphreys, P. (2004) 'Personalisation and digital technologies' *Futurelab Report*. http://www.futurelab.org.uk/research/personalisation/report_01.htm

Greene, G. (1939) *The Confidential Agent*. Vintage.

Greller, W. (2005) *E-learning and Pedagogy: A new trend in e-learning*, Presentation at University of Veterinary Science, March 2005. http://www.staff.uhi.ac.uk/wolfgang/elearningPresentation.htm

Guernsey, L. (2003) 'In the lecture hall, a geek chorus', *New York Times, 24* July 2003. http://www.nytimes.com/2003/07/24/technology/circuits/24mess.html?ex=1060315200&en=98dc374912ea9fda&ei=5070 Accessed 9th May 2006

Hampel, R. and Hauck, M. (2004) 'Towards an effective use of audio-conferencing in distance language courses', *Language Learning & Technology* 8(1) pp. 66–82.

Hansen, M., Madnick, S. and Siegel, M. (2003) 'Data integration using web services'. In Bressan, S., Chaudhri, A., Lee, M., Yu, J. and Lacroix, Z. (eds) *Efficiency and Effectiveness of XML Tools and Techniques and Data Integration over the Web*, VLDB 2002 Workshop EEXTT and CAiSE 2002 Workshop DTWeb. 'Lecture Notes in Computer Science 2590', Springer.

Harrison, M. (2004) 'eLMS: The e-learning managed solution: Enabling learning into the future', *Library Hi Tech News*, 21(7) 13–17.

Hiler, J. (2002) 'Blogs as disruptive tech', *WebCrimson*. http://www.webcrimson.com/ourstories/blogsdisruptivetech.htm

Hummel, H. G. K., Manderveld, J. M., Tattersall, C. and Koper, E. J. R. (2004) 'Educational modelling language and learning design: New opportunities for instructional reusability and personalised learning', *Int. J. Learning Technology* 1(1) pp. 111–26.

IMS (2003a) *IMS Simple Sequencing Best Practice and Implementation Guide*. http://www.imsglobal.org/simplesequencing/ssv1p0/imsss_bestv1p0.html

IMS (2003b) *IMS Learning Design Best Practice and Implementation Guide*. http://www.imsglobal.org/learningdesign/ldv1p0/imsld_bestv1p0.html

IMS (2005a) *IMS e-portfolio Specification*. http://www.imsglobal.org/ep/index.html

IMS (2005b) *Content Packaging Specification*. http://www.imsglobal.org/content/packaging/index.html

IMS (2006a) *IMS Question & Test Interoperability Specification*. http://www.imsglobal.org/question/index.html

IMS (2006b) *Tools Interoperability Guidelines*. http://www.imsglobal.org/ti/index.html

Jackson, J. (2003) 'Disruptive technologies', *Washington Technology*, 27 January 2003, 17(20). http://www.washingtontechnology.com/news/17_20/cover-stories/19859–1.html

JISC (Joint Information Systems Committee) (2000) *Circular 7/00: MLEs in further education: progress report*. JISC 1 July 2000. http://www.jisc.ac.uk/index.cfm?name=news_circular_7_00

JISC (Joint Information Systems Committee) (2003) *Portals: Frequently asked questions*. http://www.jisc.ac.uk/index.cfm?name=ie_portalsfaq

Jorgensen, N. (2001) 'Putting it all in the trunk: Incremental software development in the FreeBSD project', *Information Systems Journal* 11 pp. 321–36.

Jupiter Research (2003) Beyond the Personalization Myth: Cost-effective alternatives to influence intent. Jupiter Research Corporation.

Kraan, W. (2003a) 'Learning Design inspiration', *CETIS News*. http://www.cetis.ac.uk/content2/20031105152011

Kraan, W. (2003b) 'The teachers teach the techies', *CETIS news*, 15 April 2003. http://www.cetis.ac.uk/content/20030415235439

Kraan, W. (2004) *CETIS Quarterly Newsletter*, CETIS, 8 October 2004.

Kreijns, K., Kirschner, P. A. and Jochems, W. (2002) 'The sociability of computer-supported collaborative learning environments', *Educational Technology & Society*, 5(1). http://ifets.ieee.org/periodical/vol_1_2002/kreijns.html

Land, R. and Bayne, S. (2004) 'Screen or monitor? Surveillance and disciplinary power in online learning environments'. In Land, R. and Bayne, S. (eds) *Education in Cyberspace*. RoutledgeFalmer.

Laurillard, D. and McAndrew, P. (2003) 'Reusable educational software: A basis for generic e-learning tasks'. In Littlejohn, A. (ed) *Resources for Networked Learning*. Kogan Page.

Laurillard, D., Stratford, M., Luckin, R., Plowman, L., and Taylor, J. (2000) 'Affordances for learning in a non-linear narrative medium', *Journal of Interactive Media in Education* 2. http://www-jime.open.ac.uk/00/2/Laurillord-00–2.pdf

LeAP Project Case Study (2004) *Implementing Web Services in an Education Environment.* Version Date: 20 July 2004. http://www.education.tas.gov.au/admin/ict/projects/imsdoecasestudy/LeAPProjectCase.pdf

LeMay, R. (2005) 'Blogging censorship gains support', *CNET News*, 13 April 2005. http://news.com.com/Blog+censorship+gains+support/2100–1028_3–5670096.html

Liber, O. and Holyfield, S. (eds) (2006) 'Creating a managed learning environment', *JISC InfoNet.* http://www.jiscinfonet.ac.uk/InfoKits/InfoKits/creating-an-mle/index_html

McAndrew, P., Goodyear, P., and Dalziel, J. (2006) 'Patterns, designs and activities: Unifying descriptions of learning structures', *International Journal of Learning Technology* 2(2), 216–42.

McCloskey, D. N. (1990) 'Storytelling in economics'. In Nash, C. (ed) *Narrative in Culture: The uses of storytelling in the sciences, philosophy, and literature*, pp. 5–22. Routledge.

McConnell, D. (1994) *Implementing Computer Supported Cooperative Learning*. Kogan Page.

McGrenere, J. and Ho, W. (2000) 'Affordances: Clarifying and evolving a concept', *Proceedings of Graphics Interface,* May, Montreal. http://www.dgp.utoronto.ca/~joanna/papers/gi_2000_affordances.pdf

McLuhan, M. (1962) *The Gutenberg Galaxy*. University of Toronto Press.

McMullin, B. and Munro, M. (2004) *Moodle at DCU.* http://odtl.dcu.ie/wp/2004/odtl-2004–01.html

Martin, Y. M. and Karmel, T. (2002) 'Expansion in higher education during the 1990s: effects on access and student quality', *Department of Education, Science and Training, Australia.* http://www.dest.gov.au/sectors/higher_education/publications_resources/profiles/expansion_in_higher_education_during_the_1990s.htm

Morrisson, D. (2005) 'The virtual learning environment takes it personally', 16 December 2005. http://www.bath.ac.uk/dacs/cdntl/pMachine/morriblog_comments.php?id=P497_0_4_0

Muschamp, P. (2004) 'An introduction to Web Services', *BT Technology Journal* 22(1) pp. 9–18.

Nicholson, S. (2002) 'Socialization in the "virtual hallway": Instant messaging in the asynchronous web-based distance education classroom', *The Internet and Higher Education* 5(4) pp. 363–72. http://bibliomining.com/nicholson/virthall.html

Noble, D. (1998) 'Digital diploma mills, part I: The automation of higher education', *FirstMonday* 3(1). http://www.firstmonday.dk/issues/issue3_1/noble/

Norman, D. (1988) *The Psychology of Everyday Things*. Basic Books.

Norman, D. (1998) *The Invisible Computer.* MIT Press.

O'Reilly, T. (2005) *What is Web 2.0? Design Patterns and Business Models for the Next Generation of Software*. http://www.oreillynet.com/pub/a/oreilly/tim/news/2005/09/30/what-is-web-20.html

OECD (2005) 'E-learning in tertiary education: Where do we stand?' *Education & Skills 2005* 4, pp. 1–293.

Paulsen, M. F. (2002) *Online Education Systems: Discussion and definition of terms*. http://www.nettskolen.com/forskning/Definition%20of%20Terms.pdf

Pemberton, L. and Griffiths, R. (1998) 'The timeless way: Making living cooperative buildings with design patterns'. In *Cooperative Buildings: Integrating information, organization, and architecture. Proceedings of the First International Workshop, CoBuild'98, Darmstadt, Germany, February 1998*, Lecture Notes in Computer Science. Springer, pp. 142–53.

Perec, G. (1978) *Life: A user's manual*. Vintage.

Pew Internet and American Life Project (2001) *Teenage Life Online: The rise of the instant-message generation and the internet's impact on friendships and family relationships*. http://www.pewinternet.org/report_display.asp?r=36

Prensky, M. (2001) 'Digital natives, digital immigrants', *On the Horizon*. NCB University Press, 9(5). http://www.marcprensky.com/writing/Prensky%20-%20Digital%20Natives,%20Digital%20Immigrants%20-%20Part1.pdf

Raymond, E. (2001) *The Cathedral and the Bazaar*. O'Reilly. http://www.catb.org/~esr/writings/cathedral-bazaar/cathedral-bazaar/

Richardson, H. C. and Ward, R. (2005) 'Developing and implementing a methodology for reviewing e-portfolio products', *Report for JISC*. http://www.jisc.ac.uk/uploaded_documents/epfr.doc

Riggs, W. and von Hippel, E. (1994) 'Incentives to innovate and the sources of innovation: The case of scientific instruments', *Research Policy* 23(4) pp. 459–69.

Rogers, E. M. (1962) *Diffusion of Innovations*. The Free Press.

Sadler, R. (1989) 'Formative assessment and the design of instructional systems', *Instructional Science* 18 pp. 119–44.

Salmon, G. (2004) *E-moderating: The key to teaching and learning online*. RoutledgeFalmer.

Schon, D. (1983) *The Reflective Practitioner: How professionals think in action*. Basic Books.

Sharples, M. (2003) 'Disruptive devices: Mobile technology for conversational learning', *International Journal of Continuing Engineering Education and Lifelong Learning* 12(5) pp. 504–20. http://www.nottingham.ac.uk/lsri/msh/Papers/ijceell.pdf

Skidmore, D. (2005) 'The future of software as a business artifact', *Proceedings of First International Conference on Open Source Systems*, Geneva, pp. 231–36.

Smissen, I., McKnight, S. and Coldwell, J. (2003) 'Why WebCT Vista @ Deakin?' *4th Annual WebCT Asia Pacific Conference*, Queensland Australia, September 2003. http://www.webct.com/asiapacific03/viewpage?name=asiapacific03_programmes

Stamelos, I., Angelis, L., Oikonomou, A. and Bleris, G. (2002) 'Code quality analysis in open source software development', *Information Systems Journal* 12 pp. 43–60.

Sternberg, E. (1997) 'The defects of stakeholder theory', *Corporate Governance: An international review* 5(1) pp. 3–10.

SUNY Learning Network (2005) *Technology Strategy Report*. http://le.suny.edu/sln/rpc/sln2tsr.pdf

Suriowecki J (2004) *The Wisdom of Crowds: Why the many are smarter than the few and how collective wisdom shapes business, economies, societies and nations*. Little, Brown.

Tanenbaum, D. (2003) 'OSS Watch Scoping Study'. *OSS-watch*. http://www.oss-watch.ac.uk/studies/scoping/

UK LOM Core (2004) http://www.cetis.ac.uk/profiles/uklomcore

von Hippel, E. (2005) *Democratizing Innovation*. MIT Press.

WebCT (2003) *Access, Quality and Cost: E-learning's contribution*. http://www.webct.com/service/viewcontentframe?contentID=17982696

Weber, S. (2004) *The Success of Open Source*. Harvard University Press

Wegerif, R. (1998) 'The social dimension of asynchronous learning networks', *Journal of Asynchronous Learning Networks*, 2(1). http://www.sloan-c.org/publications/jaln/v2n1/v2n1_wegerif.asp

Weller, M., Pegler, C. and Mason, R. (2005) 'Students' experience of component versus integrated virtual learning environments', *Journal of Computer Assisted Learning* 21(4) pp. 253–9(7).

Weller, M. J. (2002) *Delivering Learning on the Net: The why, what and how of online education*. RoutledgeFalmer.

Wijekumar, K. J., Meyer, B., Wagoner, D. and Ferguson, L. (2006) 'Technology affordances: The real story in research with K-12 and undergraduate learners', *British Journal of Educational Technology* 37(2) pp. 191–210.

Wyles, R. (2004) 'Evaluation of Learning Management System software: Part II of LMS evaluation', *Open Source e-Learning Environment and CommunityPlatform Project*. http://eduforge.org/docman/view.php/7/17/Evaluation%20of%20LMS%20-%20Part%20II.pdf

Wyles, R. (2005) *New Zealand Open Source Virtual Learning Environment Project*. http://eduforge.org/docman/view.php/7/240/NZOSVLE1.ppt

Index